# Rhythm in Modern Poetry

## COGNITION, POETICS, AND THE ARTS

The **Cognition, Poetics, and the Arts** series fosters high-quality interdisciplinary research at the intersection of the cognitive sciences and the arts that focuses on cognitive approaches to literatures, arts, and cultures from around the world with three major objectives: (1) to develop theories and methodologies that further our understanding of the arts as central and complex operations of human minding; (2) to investigate the ways models of minding and artistic creation and reception have been developed and revised in relation to each other throughout history and in different cultural contexts; and (3) to develop theoretical and methodological understandings of how the arts illuminate and contribute to the cognitive sciences.

### Series Editors
Alexander Bergs, University of Osnabrück, Germany
Margaret H. Freeman, Myrifield Institute for Cognition and the Arts, USA
Peter Schneck, University of Osnabrück, Germany

### Volumes in the Series:
*Emily Dickinson's Poetic Art: A Cognitive Reading,* by Margaret H. Freeman
*Rhythm in Modern Poetry: An Essay in Cognitive Versification Studies,*
by Eva Lilja
*Cognition in the Poem: Processes of Subjectivity in Comparative Poetics,*
by Victor Bermúdez (forthcoming)
*European Churches and Chinese Temples as Neuro-Theatrical Sites,*
by Mark Pizzato (forthcoming)

# Rhythm in Modern Poetry

## An Essay in Cognitive Versification Studies

Eva Lilja

BLOOMSBURY ACADEMIC
NEW YORK • LONDON • OXFORD • NEW DELHI • SYDNEY

BLOOMSBURY ACADEMIC
Bloomsbury Publishing Inc, 1385 Broadway, New York, NY 10018, USA
Bloomsbury Publishing Plc, 50 Bedford Square, London, WC1B 3DP, UK
Bloomsbury Publishing Ireland, 29 Earlsfort Terrace, Dublin 2, D02 AY28, Ireland

BLOOMSBURY, BLOOMSBURY ACADEMIC and the Diana logo
are trademarks of Bloomsbury Publishing Plc

First published in the United States of America 2024
Paperback edition published 2025

Copyright © Eva Lilja, 2024

'The Fury of Rain Storms' and 'Knee Song' from *The Complete Poems* by Anne Sexton. Copyright © 1981 by Linda Gray Sexton and Loring Conant, Jr., executors of the will of Anne Sexton. Foreword copyright © 1981 by Maxine Kumin. Used by permission of HarperCollins Publishers.

Reprinted by permission of SLL/Sterling Lord Literistic, Inc.
Copyright by Anne Sexton, c/o Linday Sexton, Literary Executor.

For legal purposes the List of figures on pp. ix–x and Acknowledgements on pp. xvii–xix constitute an extension of this copyright page.

Cover design by Tjasa Krivec and Eleanor Rose
Cover image © John Greim / Getty Images

All rights reserved. No part of this publication may be: i) reproduced or transmitted in any form, electronic or mechanical, including photocopying, recording or by means of any information storage or retrieval system without prior permission in writing from the publishers; or ii) used or reproduced in any way for the training, development or operation of artificial intelligence (AI) technologies, including generative AI technologies. The rights holders expressly reserve this publication from the text and data mining exception as per Article 4(3) of the Digital Single Market Directive (EU) 2019/790.

Bloomsbury Publishing Inc does not have any control over, or responsibility for, any third-party websites referred to or in this book. All internet addresses given in this book were correct at the time of going to press. The author and publisher regret any inconvenience caused if addresses have changed or sites have ceased to exist, but can accept no responsibility for any such changes.

Whilst every effort has been made to locate copyright holders the publishers would be grateful to hear from any person(s) not here acknowledged.

Library of Congress Cataloging-in-Publication Data
Names: Lilja, Eva, 1943- author.
Title: Rhythm in modern poetry : an essay in cognitive versification studies / Eva Lilja.
Description: New York : Bloomsbury Academic, 2023. | Series: Cognition, poetics, and the arts | Includes bibliographical references and index. |
Summary: "A pioneering work in cognitive versification studies, scrutinizing the rhythmical means of free verse"– Provided by publisher.
Identifiers: LCCN 2023013068 (print) | LCCN 2023013069 (ebook) | ISBN 9798765100967 (hardback) | ISBN 9798765100974 (paperback) | ISBN 9798765100998 (pdf) | ISBN 9798765100981 (epub) | ISBN 9798765101001 (ebook other)
Subjects: LCSH: English poetry–History and criticism. | Poetry, Modern–History and criticism. | Cognition in literature. | Versification. | Modernism (Literature) |
LCGFT: Literary criticism.
Classification: LCC PR502 .L45 2023 (print) | LCC PR502 (ebook) |
DDC 808.1–dc23/eng/20230601
LC record available at https://lccn.loc.gov/2023013068
LC ebook record available at https://lccn.loc.gov/2023013069

ISBN: HB: 979-8-7651-0096-7
PB: 979-8-7651-0097-4
ePDF: 979-8-7651-0099-8
eBook: 979-8-7651-0098-1

Series: Cognition, Poetics, and the Arts

Typeset by Integra Software Services Pvt. Ltd.

For product safety related questions contact productsafety@bloomsbury.com.

To find out more about our authors and books visit www.bloomsbury.com and sign up for our newsletters.

*For my lovely and talented daughter*
*Professor Mona Lilja*

# Contents

List of figures — ix
Preface — xi
Foreword by Margaret H. Freeman — xii
Acknowledgements — xvii

Introduction — 1

Part 1  The poetic gestalt — 15

1  Verse systems and principles of rhythm — 17
2  The rhythmic gestalt — 27
3  Rhythm and significance — 39
4  Temporal and spatial rhythms: The intermedia perspective — 51
5  Cognitive versification theory: Some aspects — 63
6  Levels and times — 75

Part 2  Reading free verse rhythms — 87

7  Cognitive economy — 89
8  The poem in the body — 101
9  Patterns of culture — 113
10  Direction — 125
11  Balance in versification — 139
12  Rhythm in modern poetry — 151

References — 155
Index — 163

# Figures

| | | |
|---|---|---|
| 0.1 | Carmen's motion is backwards and upwards. 2012. Photo © Nobu Yamamoto | 3 |
| 0.2 | Tightrope walker Helena Kågermark. 2011. Photo © Michael Hopsch | 10 |
| 0.3 | Looking back, using space, augmenting room. 2012. Photo © Nobu Yamamoto | 12 |
| 1.1 | Carmen's dance forms sequences in a dynamic play. However, ballroom dancing follows the serial principle. Seriality overruns the now and the gestalt might go on forever, as all devoted dancers know. 2012. Photo © Nobu Yamamoto | 18 |
| 2.1 | Line lengths and SSR for 'The Fury of Rain Storms' | 33 |
| 3.1 | Wassily Kandinsky, 'Composition 8', 1923. © 2022. The Solomon R. Guggenheim Foundation/Art Resource, NY/ Scala, Florence | 41 |
| 4.1 | Cognitive schemas in time and space. Lena Hopsch and Eva Lilja. 2010. With permission by Michael Hopsch | 54 |
| 4.2 | Wassily Kandinsky, 'Gelb – Rot – Blau', 1925. © 2022. Photo Josse/Scala, Florence | 55 |
| 4.3 | Sylvia Plath's poem inserted in triangles and squares by Lena Hopsch. 2010. With permission by Michael Hopsch | 60 |
| 5.1 | Facsimile of Lawrence Ferlinghetti, *A Coney Island of the Mind*, 1958. New Directions. Copyright © 1958 by Lawrence Ferlinghetti. Reprinted by permission of New Directions Publishing Corp | 66 |
| 5.2 | Facsimile of a Ferlinghetti poem with directions inserted by Lena Hopsch. 1958, 2010. With permission by Michael Hopsch and New Directions | 70 |
| 5.3 | Balance and tension in squares. By Lena Hopsch. 2010. With permission by Michael Hopsch | 72 |
| 5.4 | Interrelation between precategorial listening and form/meaning. 2003. Danish original by Ole Kühl, expanded and translated. Reproduced with permission | 73 |
| 8.1 | Dancing can be irregular jumps. 2012. Photo © Nobu Yamamoto | 110 |

10.1 Looking backwards. In this picture, the centre of gravity lies to the left but Carmen's bottom and feet to the right also takes place. 2012. Photo © Nobu Yamamoto    129

10.2 Carmen takes a stride in a forward falling movement, almost at the limit of losing control. The French word 'enjambment' could be translated 'to stride'. 2012. Photo © Nobu Yamamoto    130

10.3 Hermes on the run. Umberto Boccioni, 'Unique Forms of Continuity'. 1913. Reproduced courtesy of Metropolitan Museum of Art. Bequest of Lydia Winston Malbin, 1989    137

11.1 Umberto Boccioni, 'Development of a Bottle in Space'. 1913. Compare with Boccioni's interpretation of Hermes dashing through the heavens in Figure 10.3. Reproduced courtesy of Metropolitan Museum of Art. Bequest of Lydia Winston Malbin, 1989    140

11.2 Axis balance and twin pan balance. The arrows mark how forces influence the balance points. Mark Johnson, *The Body in the Mind*, 1987: 86. Reproduced with permission from University of Chicago Press    142

11.3 Axis balance, or approximately standing still. Forms in a perceived equivalence point at the bodily experience of walking. Carmen's axis is her own backbone. The salience of the irregularity of Carmen's bent knee makes the balance extra expressive. As said in Chapter 7, a small asymmetry creates better reader attention than complete similarity. 2012. Photo © Nobu Yamamoto    145

# Preface

The very beginning of this book took place sixty years ago on a lovely May evening, when I, as a young student, for the first time read Edgar Lee Masters' *Spoon River* anthology. It was something odd with his versification. Free verse, yes, however full of irregular rhymes and weird rhythmic figures. What did they do to the sad stories about Spoon River people? In my dissertation some years later, I tried to understand how free verse works. I discovered its proud history and named its different devices. I have returned to the subject over and over again, and with every new book I went deeper into the delicacy of the verse.

Later on, I met Reuven Tsur, the father of cognitive poetics. This was a decisive meeting, and now I had the bones for my verse theories. He determinedly included form questions in his poetics, and with him versification studies have developed into a main study of the cognitive poetics field. Now he is gone, but we can continue his work.

Professional inspiration is important. However, I could do nothing without the support of my family, in particular my partner Åke Johansson and my daughter Professor Mona Lilja at Global Studies in Gothenburg with whom I always can discuss scholarly questions as well as daily problems. As a token of my gratitude, I dedicate this book to Mona. The cream of days are my sweet grandchildren.

Kärradal & Göteborg, Summer 2022<br>Eva Lilja

# Foreword

Margaret H. Freeman
*Myrifield Institute for Cognition and the Arts*

For centuries in the Western tradition, it was assumed that body, mind, and soul were separate entities. Although Giambattista Vico's *La Scienzia Nuova* in the eighteenth century challenged the Cartesian notion of a body–mind split, and the rise of evolutionary theory and scientists such as George Henry Lewes in his works *The Physical Basis of Mind* and *The Problems of Life and Mind* conceived alternate theories in the nineteenth century, it was not until the twentieth century that scholars began to explore, both theoretically and methodologically, the implications of embodied cognition; that the processes of minding are generated by the integration of brain and body. Much work has already been accomplished in interdisciplinary research involving the neurosciences, the arts, biology, linguistics, literature, psychology, anthropology, sociology, and so on, and much still needs to be done. This is especially true in the somewhat neglected area of research into the cognitive bases of biorhythms in modern poetry.

As Benzon (2006: 8) notes: 'Our task as literary critics in the age of the cognitive and neurosciences is to not explicate what individual texts mean, but to understand how they shape the experience of reading.' In doing so, he concludes:

> [O]nly a biological approach to the arts will allow us to understand how the shared pleasures of aesthetic activity are the foundation of our humanity. Those pleasures are grounded in the intrinsic dynamic patterns of the human nervous system, in its capacity for pattern and design. Literary works are the product of those capacities as well and literary form is their direct trace.
>
> (2006: 27)

This volume by Professor Lilja is exemplary in that regard, with its focus on the biological rhythms of our bodies as they are expressed through various arts including dance, sculpture, visual art, and especially poetry. Building on the findings by researchers in versification studies, especially work on poetic rhythm by Derek Attridge, Richard Cureton, and Reuven Tsur, Professor Lilja provides a unified theory and methodology for understanding rhythm in modern 'free verse' poetry that includes:

1. historical background;
2. relation of the various strands of influence from different language poetic traditions;
3. interrelationship of verse systems and the principles of rhythm;
4. cognitive versification theory;
5. cultural patterns; and
6. bodily basis of aesthetic rhythm.

None of these concerns, even at the most general level, are featured in recent handbooks and encyclopedias that deal with literary studies or cognition (see the listing below of works consulted). Poetry and prosody are given only passing mention, if at all, and meter and rhythm not at all. When poetry is featured to any extent, it occurs (with reference to the work of Reuven Tsur) in an essay on autism in *The Oxford Handbook of Cognitive Literary Studies* (Savarese 2015). The *Britannica*'s entry mentions the physiological basis of rhythm but refers only to linguistic aspects:

> In free verse, rhythm most commonly arises from the arrangement of linguistic elements into patterns that more nearly approximate the natural cadence of speech and that give symmetry to the verse. The rhythmical resources available to free verse include syntactical patterning; systematic repetition of sound, words, phrases, and lines; and the relative value of temporal junctures occasioned by caesura (a marked pause in the middle of a line), line length, and other determinants of pace.
> 
> (www.britannica.com/art/rhythm-poetry)

References to researchers in the principles of meter and rhythm like Derek Attridge and Richard Cureton are not mentioned. In my own article on cognitive poetics in *The Oxford Handbook of Cognitive Linguistics* (Freeman 2007: 1192–1193), I noted:

> Cureton ... and Tsur ... both challenge Cognitive Linguistics' failure to attend to the formal aspects of literary works, such as the temporal dimension of meter and rhythm. Although differing in their theories of rhythm, both believe that rhythm is a general cognitive process and make significant claims about the formal and prosodic features of poetry that need to be explored in order to fully account for the role of rhythm in human cognition and language.

The 'Rhythm' entry in the first edition of *The Princeton Encyclopedia of Poetry and Poetics* (1965) is simply a cross-reference to the more general subject of prosody. By its fourth edition (2012), 'Rhythm' received its own entry, and addresses its cognitive significance as follows (Attridge 2012: 1195):

> One cannot understand rhythm without considering its realization in human psychology and physiology; as readers of poetry, it is the *experience* of rhythm that is important to us, and this experience is both mental and bodily. At its most basic, rhythm is a patterning of energy, of tension and release, movement and countermovement that we both perceive and produce—or reproduce—in our own brains and muscles.

Attridge concludes: 'There is still much that is not fully understood about the operation of rhythm in verse, and its relation to the rhythms of lang. and of music, and to rhythm itself as a perceptual phenomenon' (1197–1198).

Professor Lilja's research is therefore especially welcome in addressing the significance of rhythmic movements in embodied cognition. An emerita professor at the University of Gothenburg, her long career in researching and teaching the elements of rhythm in poetic cognition places her in a unique position of being able to clarify and explain how the principles of modern versification emerged from several different strands in the European poetic tradition. In 1986, together with Kristian Wåhlin, she founded NordMetrik, a society for metrical studies. Its latest international conference pre-pandemic was held in Stockholm in September 2018.

Professor Lilja's publications explore and extend her 1981 dissertation at the University of Gothenburg on *Studies in Swedish Free Verse*, culminating in the publication of *Swedish Metrics* in 2006, a standard book in versification covering theory, history, and practical methodology, written in cooperation with the Language Committee of the Swedish Academy. Her articles include work in cultural and gender studies as well as monographs about Swedish poets. In 2014, Professor Lilja adopted a more explicit cognitive approach in her 2014 book, *Poesiens Rytmik*, written for Scandinavian poets. This book became the basis for translating its principles into English with a more historical and scholarly focus.

Because it embraces the emergence of the principles in free verse throughout the European tradition, *Rhythm in Modern Poetry: An Essay in Cognitive Versification Studies* is the first comprehensive account of the emergence of English free verse from the historical background of various verse systems emerging from Ancient Greek versification, the medieval four-beat line, and the Bible. As a result, it clarifies and deepens our understanding of the rhythmic principles of modern English poetic forms. In addition, it provides an extensive account of the physiological and cognitive bases of rhythm in general, including both temporal and spatial aspects such as movement, direction, balance, prolongation, repetition, and patterning of serial, sequential, and dynamic rhythms.

The book is divided into two parts. The first, Chapters 1–6, 'The Poetic Gestalt,' takes the reader through the technical aspects of understanding the historical emergence of the general cognitive principles of modernist verse rhythm. By focusing not simply on the metalinguistic features in poetry but how they are shaped by and related to the general rhythms inherent in our bodily movements and expressed in other art forms such as dance, sculpture, and the visual arts, Professor Lilja provides a more comprehensive account of the underlying cognitive processes of the temporal and spatial forms of force dynamics, patterning, and balance. The second, Chapters 7–12, 'Reading Free Verse Rhythms,' applies the rhythmic principles outlined in the first part to discussions of how to read free verse from these perspectives with examples from several English poets.

As a result, Professor Lilja's contribution to an understanding of the physiological bases of rhythm as they are expressed through poetry and the arts is of immense importance to extending the interdisciplinary reaches of the cognitive sciences and embodied cognition. For those readers interested in the workings of free verse, it provides detailed and specific guidance on how to read the rhythms of modern poetry.

## References

*[Citations to the work of Attridge, Cureton, and Tsur, among others, may be found in the book's general References.]*

Attridge, D. (2012), 'Rhythm', in *The Princeton Encyclopedia of Poetry and Poetics*, 4th edn, edited by Stephen Cushman, Clare Cavanagh, Jahan Ramazani, and Paul Rouzer, Princeton, NJ: Princeton University Press.

Benzon, W. L. (2006), 'Literary Morphology: Nine Propositions in a Naturalist Theory of Form', *PsyArt: An Online Journal for the Psychological Study of the Arts*, article 060608.

Burke, M., ed. (2014), *The Routledge Handbook of Stylistics*, London and New York: Routledge.

Freeman, M. H. (2007), 'Cognitive Linguistic Approaches to Literary Studies: State of the Art in Cognitive Poetics', in *The Oxford Handbook of Cognitive Linguistics*, edited by Dirk Geeraerts and Hubert Cuyckens, 1175–1202, Oxford: Oxford University Press.

Lewes, G. H. (1879), *Problems of Life and Mind: The Study of Psychology—Its Object, Scope, and Method*, London: Trübner & Co., Ludgate Hill.

Lewes, G. H. (1893), *The Physical Basis of Mind*, London: Kegan Paul.

Newen, A., L. De Bruin, and S. Gallagher, eds. 2018. *The Oxford Handbook of 4E Cognition*, Oxford: Oxford University Press.

Savarese, R. J. (2015), 'What Some Autistics Can Teach Us about Poetry: A Neurocosmopolitan Approach', in *The Oxford Handbook of Cognitive Literary Studies*, edited by Lisa Zunshine, 393–420, Oxford: Oxford University Press.

Vico, G. (1948[1744]), *The New Science of Giambattista Vico* (Principi di scienza nuova d'intorno alla communinatura delle nazioni), translated by Max Harold Fisch and Thomas Goddard Bergin, Ithaca, NY: Cornell University Press.

# Acknowledgements

Over the years, a number of different contexts have been crucial in the writing of this book. The first was created with Kristian Wåhlin and Eddy Otterloo at the faculty of Humanities at Gothenburg University when we were young PhDs. Together we took the initiative to form a research environment: *The Nordic Society for Metrical Studies [NordMetrik]*. For over thirty years, we collected Scandinavian metrists for scholarly discussions and published sixteen books of preliminaries. Around 2010, the Society became international. Today it is based in Oslo, where Professor Sissel Furuseth continues to publish the *NordMetrik Newsletter*.

Within *NordMetrik*, two people, Lena Hopsch and Rudolf Rydstedt, helped me to move beyond the group. I would like to express my sincerest thanks to both of them. Together, the three of us developed the basic structure of the versification theory on which this book is based. Rudolf's erudition in the field made him a veritable dictionary of cognitive poetics. Lena was initially a sculptor and knew almost everything about spatial rhythms. However, she sadly passed away, and I have to thank her husband and copyright owner Michael Hopsch for generously letting me use her work even today. The musician and semiotician Ole Kühl in Århus, Denmark, allowed me to use his findings about musical rhythm.

A second important context for me has been the Swedish Academy, when they employed me to write the Swedish standard work in metrics, *Svensk Metrik [Swedish Metrics]* (2006). My back-up group of Academy members – Professors Sture Allén, Göran Malmqvist, Bo Ralph, and Gunnel Vallquist – showed me, among other things, what true erudition can mean; erudition that they generously shared. However, the rhythm chapter never found its form in the handbook, and later on I started basic research on this theme, seeking to find out what poetic rhythm is really about. A first presentation of the results was made in *Poesiens Rytmik [The Rhythmics of Poetry]* (2014).

A third context of great importance for me has been the international one. Christoph Küper's versification conferences in Vechta meant interesting contacts and collaborations. So did the Tartu group and the journal *Studia Metrica et Poetica* lead by Maria Lotman. The Poetics and Linguistics Association (PALA) contributed to the development of cognitive poetics as well as in metrics. I would also like to thank Professor Mick Short for an interesting stay in Lancaster in 2007. The breakthrough of cognitive poetics took place with a conference in Osnabrück in 2013 organized by Alexander Bergs. Several scholars, not least Reuven Tsur and Margaret Freeman, inspired and influenced me a lot. Reuven, who left us in 2021, was always willing to answer my questions, and Margaret has done me the great favour of reading the manuscript of this book. Many thanks!

In this book, you will find many pictures of the dancer Carmen Olsson. As a butoh dancer she used to perform in Japan. The skilled photographer Nobu Yamamoto caught her moving at Yoshino River, and he has generously allowed me to reproduce his pictures. My deepest thanks to Carmen and Nobu.

Not a native speaker, I needed someone to control my notations, and I thank Anna Casanova for this task. Last but not least I will thank the Bloomsbury editorial team, Hali Han and Amy Martin, who has facilitated the work on this book in more ways than I can remember.

An earlier version of Chapter 8 appeared as 'Embodied Rhythm in Space and Time' by Lena Hopsch and Eva Lilja in *Style* 51 (2017): 413–41.

Concerning Leonard Cohen, 'No 55' in *The Energy of Slaves,* copyright 1972, every attempt to secure permissions to publish this poem has been made. If in any case credits or copyrights are not accurate, the error should be brought directly to the attention of the publisher.

Lawrence Ferlinghetti, '"Sweet and various the woodlark" #13' from *A Coney Island of the Mind,* ©1958. Reprinted by permission of New Directions Publishing Corp.

Seamus Heaney, 'Night Drive' and 'Sloe Gin' in *Open Ground: Selected Poems 1966-96* copyright © 1998. Reprinted with kind permission from Faber and Faber Ltd. and Farrar, Straus, and Giroux.

Ted Hughes, 'Perfect Light' in *Birthday Letters* copyright © 1998. Reprinted with permission from Faber and Faber Ltd. and Farrar, Straus, and Giroux.

Paul Muldoon, 'Moore Geese' in *Maggot* copyright © 2010. Reprinted with permission from Faber and Faber Ltd. and Farrar, Straus, and Giroux.

Sylvia Plath, 'Poppies in October' and 'Winter Trees' in *Collected Poems* copyright © 1981. Reprinted with permission from Faber and Faber Ltd. and HarperCollins Publishers.

*Acknowledgements*

Ann Sexton, 'Knee Song' and 'The Fury of Rain Storms' from *The Complete Poems* copyright © 1981 by Linda Gray Sexton and Loring Conant, Jr., executors of the will of Anne Sexton. Foreword copyright © 1981 by Maxine Kumin. Reprinted with permission from HarperCollins Publishers and SLL/Sterling Lord Literistic, Inc.

# Introduction

## *Mousikē*

In his dialogue *The Laws*, Plato defines rhythm in terms of 'ordered movement'. With this, he refers to the dancing body moving in time as well as in space. In the theatres of ancient Athens, the dancing choir in the orchestra moved and recited at the same time. The Greeks did not differentiate between art forms the way we do today, instead regarding them as one and the same, something they called *mousikē* (Johnson 1987: 80, 88; Lonsdale 1992: 6).

Poetry exists as sound and as visual. Reading a poem aloud creates a temporal sequence of sounds that follow one after the other. Modern poetry, however, is mostly read silently but, even so, one hears the sounds of the poem in one's head (Linde 1974: 40, Starr 2013: 91). In that process, the reader is also aware of the printed picture, of how the poem patterns the paper. Nevertheless, I want to claim that, in poetry, temporal rhythm is more important than spatial rhythm. In older times, poetry was almost always performed, which is why rhythm and sound had to be adapted to the requirements of orality. In our time, some poetry is oral, while other texts are geared to exploiting the possibilities of the paper's surface or maybe that of the screen. Mainstream modern poems make use of both temporal and spatial rhythms, although in the poems I am concerned with in this book, temporal rhythms are primary.

Another precondition for verse rhythm is the fact that poems are made of language. The articulation of speech is studied in phonetics, which investigates the physiology of pronunciation and the lines of sound waves. Reading a poem aloud, among other things, produces frequencies and exercises the tongue. A poem might be measured as acoustic waves of pitch and air pressure. However, what one hears does not always agree exactly with that which is measured. Something happens between acoustics and understanding: a kind of patterning. Sight and hearing change the physical facts ever so slightly, increasing contrasts and making the course of sound more salient. It seems as if the rhythm of the poem emerges in co-operation between acoustic facts and human perception patterns (Johnson 1987; Lilja 2006: 81).

So far, poetic rhythm appears to be a perceptual experience; one that is based on acoustic circumstances and ordered out of the formal devices of versification – pauses, repetitions, strong and weak syllables, and so on. Sounds are patterned, creating rhythm. Sound precedes meaning in poems as well as in ordinary speech: something must be heard before any signification is possible. Various times and styles have responded differently to this precondition. Modernism's free versification emanated out of an aspiration to strengthen meaning and reduce form, or at least the rules regarding form. In contrast, bold modernist movements like Dada have attempted to reinforce the sound structure so as to free as much unrestrained signification as possible.

Back to Plato, *mousikē*, and ordered movement – the moving body could be a prototype for a discussion of aesthetic rhythm, as it continuously stages the interplay between the experiences of movement and balance. In Homer's work, one finds many descriptions of dancing. Its ancient function was threefold: apart from its important role in Greek tragedy, it was a religious or social occupation, not least in the genre of chorus lyrics or dithyrambs. The music, recitation, and dance of *mousikē* constituted a unity (Evans 2016: 12; Lonsdale 1992: 6).

Indeed, there are many question marks here. How does one dance a harsh rhythmic figure as the spondee OO? Stamping? In Chapter 2, certain common Greek colons are registered, rhythmical figures that act as building blocks of ancient Greek poems (p. 31). How could these be performed while dancing? No one knows exactly, but what one does know is that this was nevertheless done. Homer prefers anapaests ooO when describing soldiers marching; a figure that, even today, suits the forward motion in marching music (Evans 2016: 16).

## Carmen

While every art form employs rhythm, the most obvious case is dance, or the dancing body. The following image presents the dancer Carmen Olsson, from Gothenburg, Sweden, performing at a 2012 workshop by the Yoshino River in Japan. In her performance called 'River's Empathy I', Carmen dances her meeting with the Japanese landscape – the river, the mountains, and the shore. A myth tells of the river god who lives in the mountain. Carmen dances in an interplay with the river god of her thoughts. Her aim is to close in on the water and at the very end she disappears into the river. Carmen's dance will illustrate more poems later on (Lilja 2014: 9).

The dance forms an interplay between body and water. Take a look in the picture: Carmen is directed to the left – or backwards, if you take the reading direction of Germanic languages into consideration. Also the water stream runs to the right. As choreographer Efva Lilja describes it, her body seems calm and is slightly bent towards the left, as if trying to find a better angle from which to look. The weight of the body is on the right foot, with the left foot lightly supported against a rock. Carmen's hair is moving behind her head. Is there a wind? Her left hand is open in the same direction that she is looking. The right hand is hesitant, closed inwardly, with the thumb and the middle finger held as if in a meditative pose. Both arms point out from the bodily centre, which expresses openness. The open left hand reinforces this sensation.

The picture shows a basic set of rhythmic possibilities, such as forward and backward directions, stability and its opposite, balance and emotions. The body is a gestalt inscribed in the bigger gestalt of the landscape, which is framed in turn by the boundaries of the picture. My own experiences tell me the significance

**Figure 0.1** Carmen's motion is backwards and upwards. 2012. Photo © Nobu Yamamoto.

of every movement – in this case, calmness and openness. As already noted, a dancing body moves in time as well as in space, and both temporal and spatial art forms make use of rhythmic possibilities. The same basic devices reappear in every art form. Music, for example, might rush forward, stop, turn away from a stressed point, and so on. A sculpture, a work of art that is more obviously related to the human body, balances its sequences into a wholeness of equilibrium; otherwise it would fall. In painting, too, parts are organized so as to create a balance between them.

Now, as other art forms use the same basic set of rhythmic possibilities, there must be similarities between dance and poetry in terms of rhythmic structure (Andrews 2017: 71–86). The poem also performs a balancing act in the course of moving in its forward direction. In all the chapters of this book, I show how the wholeness of a poem balances, while its parts may do anything they want – they can go backwards and forwards or merely stand still.

## Historical background

My subtitle for this work is *An Essay in Cognitive Versification Studies*. I will discuss rhythm in twentieth-century free versification, but the discipline usually called 'metrics' is mostly concerned with the phenomenon of metre. Free verse needs other tools and a better label. I opt for 'versification studies' when focusing on rhythmical sequences and textual dynamics. Once seen as marginal to poetry studies, versification studies now form an important field in cognitive poetics (or poetic cognition) where basic questions of aesthetics and artistic language are studied.

How did this development take place? During the last century, two semioticians dominated the versification field – Yuri Lotman and Roman Jakobson – and both of them focused on modernist poetry to traditional forms. Lotman studied signification processes, and established delicate connections between sound and meaning (Lotman 1972). Jakobson's theory of equivalence, for its part, suited the poetry of his friends, who were Russian futurists, such as Velimir Khlebnikov and Vladimir Mayakovsky (Jakobson 1960: 358).

Here, I will concentrate on Germanic verse (English, German, and Scandinavian languages). Lately, three metrists relaunched versification studies within this field, based on findings from studies within semiotics, linguistics and cognitive studies. Reuven Tsur, Derek Attridge, and Richard Cureton have introduced wider perspectives into their respective versification systems, useful also for the study of free verse.

The very master of cognitive versification studies, Reuven Tsur, has produced a vast oeuvre over the last five decades (e.g., 1992, 2003, 2008, 2009, 2012a, 2012b, 2017, 2022). He is able to explain the signification production of poetical means. In his work, he patiently uncovers layer after layer in the poem's production of significance. Every extra signification has its own technical explanation. Structures of emotion go with the structures of sound, right down to tiny phonological differences. What has earlier been called intuition is explained here in acoustic detail such as frequencies and other precategorial information. Aesthetic observations are bolstered by hard facts.

Tsur stresses the importance of the gestalt in poems, and he has modernized the old Gestalt psychology towards this purpose. By drawing upon findings from neurology combined with those from phonology, he demonstrates the continued significance of Gestalt psychology even today. Tsur's work goes further than the old Gestalt school, by exploring a new theory that has been badly needed (Tsur 2012a: 49–55, 249). The gestalt is central for free verse as well as for old measured forms.

Indeed, Tsur is a hardcore empiricist who bases his versification studies on facts; mainly phonological and psychological facts. For me, a more interesting question has been how rhythms arise in the reception of a poem. Yet, it is a true gift to be able to control every finding with Tsur's unshakable objectivity.

Attridge's work *The Rhythms of English Poetry* has functioned as a useful standard textbook. In this work he, among other things, establishes something that he terms 'beat prosody' (1982: 76–122, 324–44), what Mihail Gasparov calls accentual verse in his history of European verse forms (Gasparov 1996: 37, 275). This form has been one of the very origins of free verse. Both of the writers emphasize medieval forms, the old Germanic four-beat line, and, in the Russian context, the *dolnik* of folk poetry (Attridge 2012, 2013: 164; Gasparov 1996: 25). The versification rule prescribes the same number of beats in every line but no rules for weak syllables (Gasparov 1996: 37). Of course, such a rhythm may turn out to be rather uneven, something that attracted the founding fathers of free verse. These accentual forms have survived until today in song lyrics and other popular genres.

In his later work, Attridge investigates movement in poetry in his development of poetic cognition. He entitles his book from 2013 *Moving Words* – a poem may be understood as movement in time. Of course, he is right – a limited movement seems to be the base of any aesthetic rhythm. I will come back to this.

In choosing his title *Moving Words*, Attridge was clearly inspired by Richard Cureton's theory of four temporalities in verse rhythm. Cureton also stresses a rhythmical motion in time – the time aspect being a main idea behind his poetics as presented in *Rhythmic Phrasing in English Verse* (1992). Cureton distinguishes four levels of rhythm: pulse, grouping, prolongation and thematic rhythm. These levels form a hierarchy in which the pulse is the smallest entity of one foot, the grouped phrase comes next, while the prolongation covers about one line. All these levels have their directions and their main stresses, and the definitive rhythm of a verse line will be a combination of the different layers.

Cureton's temporalities are useful when investigating free verse. The second level, the phrase of different lengths, is the most important one of his system. This grouping level has also become the field of free-verse rhythm. Also Cureton's fourth so-called temporality, the thematic rhythm, has turned out to be especially important for modernist poetry. The first three levels of rhythm all move, but the fourth one rests. Time is spatialized – a favourite device among modernist poets.

Cureton notates his four temporalities one by one. However, I have found this to be confusing. In my own rhythm notations, I take all levels into account in the same reading. This is for practical reasons in order to bring them in line with one another.

Tsur, Attridge, and Cureton can be identified as the fathers of cognitive versification studies, as they together, and in slightly different ways, have built a theory for their successors to follow. However, a fourth achievement has been a necessary condition for the new school to emerge as well. With this I refer to Mikhail Gasparov's mapping of the verse history in his 1996 *A History of European Versification*. In this book, Gasparov identifies the various European verse systems, opening up a whole garden of different versification types for investigation. As he demonstrates, there are really many possibilities to regulate the language of poems, with the tactus of the Renaissance being only one among them.

The introduction of different verse systems may be Gasparov's most important achievement. In northern Europe and northern America, it is possible to distinguish at least four or five different verse systems. Old Norse and medieval forms relied on the accentual verse system. With the Renaissance followed a period of accentual-syllabic verse, yielding to free verse in the twentieth century. However, the syllabic system of French poetry was introduced to the Germanic languages, not least English. Moreover, one must consider the quantitative verse system of classical antiquity, even if the languages in northern Europe and northern America resist the kind of accent that it entails. The innumerable efforts to transfer the beauty of Greek poetry into Germanic languages have produced a great many unexpected forms. Free verse is one of them.

## Free verse

*Rhythm in Modern Poetry* – as this book's title indicates, this is a study of free verse forms in the Germanic languages. Free verse consists of pronounced phrases combined with elaborate pauses. A division into lines creates the most salient pause with the line break. Free verse uses many of the devices of traditional verse (e.g. rhymes) but without any general pattern.[1]

Modernist versification developed rhythms from ancient cultures (Lilja 2006: 250–74; Belfrage 1941). Examples here include Old Greek poetry (such as that of Sappho) and Old Norse rhythms (Eddaic forms); however, Biblical poetry could also be added to the list. A fourth starting point for free versification was the avant-garde of the twentieth century, which was a productive field of rhythmic experiments. Together, these sources form a beautiful landscape with few connections left to the field of metre. Free verse was thus created four times, proceeding from four different points of departure and giving us four different types of versification: the Antique type, the Nordic type, the Biblical type, and the Dada type (or avant-garde experiments) (Lilja 2006: 268):

1. The first free verse was created around the middle of the eighteenth century, in the work of Friedrich Gottlieb Klopstock (1724–1803). Klopstock's intention was to imitate antique poetic rhythms, especially the forms of Aeolic poetry – Sappho, for example – and its Latin copies. The typical devices here are short lines, enjambments, and an affluence of spondees OO. This type of free verse was used for solemn occasions.
2. Free verse was then reinvented for the second time by Heinrich Heine (1797–1856) in the early part of the nineteenth century. Heine's free verse developed from the four-beat line, the old German popular form that can be found in folk songs and medieval chronicles with roots in the Edda songs of Old Norse poetry. This kind of free verse prioritizes lines of about ten syllables ending with a full stop, with mostly two phrases per line. This form is suited for colloquial styles.

---

[1] A negative definition would be 'nonmetrical verse' (Hartman 1980: 24).

3. Walt Whitman (1819–1892) recreated free verse for the third time, at around the middle of the nineteenth century. Influenced by the Bible, he set out to imitate the Book of Psalms, with his verse form being characterized by long lines and parallelisms (Allen 1975: 215; Bradley 1939: 448). Repeated intonation curves give it a special phrasing. Such poems were well suited for recitation. However, these Bible-inspired forms are now not very common.
4. Finally, free verse was recreated once more in the early years of the twentieth century; at Cabaret Voltaire in Zürich in 1916, to be precise. The Dada group represented the first true avant-garde, consisting of young people trying to escape the Great War (World War I). The Dadaists developed the sound poem as well as the pictorial poem, creating a powerful form with vagueness in meaning. Their underlying intention was to create a new and better world (Perloff 1999).

As one can see, free versification has grown out of the most prestigious historical patterns possible – Greek poetry, the Bible, and the Edda songs. To the list I will add the experiments of avant-garde forms, starting in 1916 and prospering first in the 1960s and later around the turn of the last millennium. In the history of rhythms, the avant-garde has made important innovations, to which I will return later.

When looking at the cultures of northern Europe, the picture, however, differs somewhat. The experiments of the French symbolists took place within a syllabic verse system that relied on vague accents. Indeed, the first free verse writers in France were actually born elsewhere, and were familiar with different accents and their effects. Gustave Kahn was originally German, Stuart Merrill and Francis Vielé-Griffin came from the United States, and Marie Krysinska was born in Poland. Most of the early pioneers – among them Arthur Rimbaud, Maurice Maeterlinck, Émile Verhaeren, Charles van Lerberghe – came from Belgium and were used to the stresses of the Flemish language (Lilja Norrlind 1981: 134).

English poetry is rather peculiar in that it uses a language combining evident stresses with a heavy influence from French syllabism. My impression is that binarity – an even contrast between strong and weak syllables – is a more obvious characteristic of the English language than that of, say, the German or the Scandinavian languages; something that could then explain the English metrists' ongoing interest in binarity in versification.[2] There is, to be sure, also

---

[2] '... spoken English has an underlying tendency towards regularity ...' (Attridge 1982: 76).

a tendency towards binarity in, for example, the Swedish language, but there it is more undefined. Different languages appear to have varying relations to alternation – that is a tendency to an even binarity. Many Germanic languages are rather stiff; something that can make metered rhythm forced and unpleasant.

What is important to note in this connection is that the pioneering modernists did not want their verse to alternate. They were looking for other kinds of rhythm that slipped out of traditional tactus. Even if some of today's metrists force free verse into a kind of alternation, they go against the aesthetic will of the modernist poets who looked for kinds of rhythm other than alternation, which ended up creating free verse.

## What is rhythm?

Rhythm, I would say, is an embodied, lived experience of the production and perception of an artwork. A simple definition of 'rhythm' might be, and often has been, something like 'recurring motion', but the matter is more complicated than that. One way to answer the question of what constitutes rhythm could be found in its negation, by instead asking: What is un-rhythmic? The answer might then be, that which lacks demarcation or structure. Rhythm is absent where there is chaos and emptiness, when the direction of the composition becomes unclear and confused, with forms losing their context (Hopsch 2008: 11). One may, for example, think of the ruins of a bombed house.

The experience of rhythm displays certain basic properties regardless of the style, mode and discourse. The general meaning of the Greek word *rhythmos* is something measured and ordered. This sense of the term – measured movement, measured time – is found, for example, in Democritus in the fifth century BC. In his dialogue *The Laws*, Plato, for his part, describes the rhythm of a dancing body in terms of 'organized movement'. With this definition by Plato in mind, aesthetic rhythm could be understood as a play with temporal or spatial proportions in an artwork. In spatial art forms, rhythm concerns proportions and tensions between different parts of the picture, the sculpture or the facade. In temporal arts like music and poetry, rhythm structures the stronger and weaker parts in the course of sound. Rhythm exists in the production as well as in the reception of an artwork (Hopsch and Lilja 2013: 103–22).

Another core concept in versification studies is gestalt, as already noted in relation to Tsur's poetics (for more on this, see p. 5). Rhythm takes place within a gestalt, in which activities aiming at equilibrium clash with displacements, creating motion (Tsur 2012a: 51, 76, 83, 86, 303). The very best example of a gestalt is the human body with its distinct boundaries; the body that moves in different directions. (See Carmen's picture on p. 12.) Conflicting form elements create tension and imbalance, but the whole artefact demonstrates some kind of balance. Much of the motion in a gestalt emanates from asymmetric sequences that are imbalanced within themselves but balance each other (Starr 2013: 92).

The image of a tightrope walker may serve to clarify my perspective. Each step on the tightrope involves first losing one's balance and then regaining it. This is, in fact, what everyone does on a daily basis on firm ground. With each step, a force draws our body forward, and to avoid falling and retain our balance, that momentum must be countered. As tightrope walking shows, equilibrium is not something static; it is, instead, balance at work (Hopsch and Lilja 2017: 415).

**Figure 0.2** Tightrope walker Helena Kågermark. Photo © Michael Hopsch.

## How to read free verse

Old cadenced verse works with tactus and rhymes, devices that suit loud recitation. By the nineteenth century, silent reading became more customary with advanced literacy. Costs for printing were sinking, and the poets abandoned the old-fashioned heavy stanzas to develop the exciting new free verse. This free verse could be difficult to grasp when listening to a recitation, and in time silent reading became the usual way to experience poems.

As already said, one might need several readings to fully understand the sayings of a modern poem. It may be rather impossible to take in a whole poem the first time one sees it – mostly a modernist text is too complex for that. One has to walk around in the poem, so to say, and look again at the line before going back to the very beginning in order to repeat the point of departure, to discover an expressive paronomasia that connects two segments, and so on. Thereafter one can understand the text, when having it present in its entirety (Attridge 2013: 49). This process of *spatial reading* establishes the poem as a room of its own (Attridge 2013: 40).

Several components are in play here. Most importantly for the spatiality of a poem is 'back-structuring' – one must know the end of a segment to be able to pattern it (Tsur 2012a: 303). Poems are distinguished by repetitions concerning sound effects, themes, motives and grammatical constructs (Jakobson 1960: 358). The second occasion of a repetition hints back at the first one. Back-structuring and repetition spatialize the text, transforming it to a room where the reader walks around looking for beauty and meaning.

To a certain degree, rhythm in the free verse of modern poetry depends on the reading. This is not a problem when enjoying a good poem; however, it makes scholarly ambitions a little ambiguous – something that might be discovered in my notations of the poems in this book. I have chosen a plausible interpretation, but also discussed some other rhythmic possibilities. A lodestar for me has been to pronounce the texts as normally as possible, thereby following ordinary speech rhythm. Of course, the adequacy of this normality could be disputed. An outstanding poem may considerably complicate the reading choices, and result in something very different from ordinary speech rhythm. However, this has been my method to avoid getting lost in translation (Couper-Kuhlen 1993: 15–17).

Some reading rules must be kept, but in other cases there is a choice to be made. One category of syllables must be stressed, and others should stay unstressed.

**Figure 0.3** Looking back, using space, augmenting room. 2012. Photo © Nobu Yamamoto.

The majority of syllables cannot be manipulated if strong or weak is regulated in the language. But one also meets a category where the reader is allowed to choose whether to stress or not stress a syllable (Malmström 1968: 115). Factors to consider are things like tempo, meaning, line length, and exclusiveness. A slow tempo is always recommended and pauses should be freely emphasized.

According to ordinary speech, the reader may stress main accents of nouns, main verbs, adjectives, numerals, and some pronouns and adverbs (Malmström 1968: 113–15). Syllables of other word classes will stay unstressed – auxiliary verbs, conjunctions, articles, and some other pronouns and adverbs. Interjections like 'oh' and 'what' may be stressed or not. Word groups may suppress weaker accents to favour the group accent, like 'shout out' oO or 0O. If the poem has too many weak syllables in a row the reader may accentuate, for example, an auxiliary verb a bit more.

But also significance affects rhythm. How one understands the text will, of course, also influence how one stresses it. Sometimes a certain word or syllable must be accentuated to make it possible for us to get sense out of the text.

There are strong and weak syllables, stressed or unstressed words, but a good interpretation also needs a level of strength that is somewhere in between these.

I have notated this level of less stress with a 0 (zero). Compounds and word groups ('shout out' 0O) frequently use the zero.

I have used ordinary speech rhythm as a norm for my interpretations. However, when talking, one obviously tries to level out the time between stresses to make the sound stream more even. Natural pronunciation makes syllables longer and shorter in order to smooth out the distance between stresses (Lilja 2007: 437; Couper-Kuhlen 1993: 15–17). People who are upset often speak in cadences (Mannerheim 1991: 171). In addition, individual readers mostly have their own ideas about how much they want to conventionalize the sound flow depending on whether they want it to be smooth or uneven. According to the fashions over time, reading styles vary over epochs, aiming at the stable tactus or the precious segment (Lilja 2006: 173–75).

## Aims

This book has certain objectives. First, I demonstrate the beauty and exquisiteness of free verse and point at modernism with its creative aesthetics. Free verse has been a neglected area within versification studies. I point at the forms of Old Greek and Old Norse as patterns for free verse.

Second, I develop versification studies following the works of Attridge, Cureton, and Tsur. Basic tools like verse systems and verse principles have hardly been used at all, with the exception of Gasparov. Tsur underlines that verse rhythm is a question of perceptions and bodily experience. I will show how it originates from precategorical and premodal perceptions.

Third, I call attention to the fact that rhythm signifies, and how signification has its base in the body with its many rhythms. Every body moves in directions, however, sometimes it just balances in slow concentration loaded with feeling.

## Notation signs

To describe rhythms in poems, a notation system is needed. I will notate as follows:

| | |
|---|---|
| Stressed syllable | O |
| Phrasal focus | **O** |

| | |
|---|---|
| Unstressed syllable | o |
| Secondary stress | 0 |
| Enjambment | > |
| Phrase shift | / |
| Rising rhythms | oO oO  or  ooO ooO and so on |
| Falling rhythms | Oo Oo  or  Ooo Ooo and so on |

*The syllable stress ratio,* SSR (Hrushovski 1954: 244, 251) tells us whether the weight of the phrase or line is heavy or light, determined by the dominance of stressed or weak syllables. The normal relationship in ordinary speech is one or two weak syllables per stress. When all syllables of the line are stressed, the ratio is 1, when half of them are stressed it is 2, and so on. The ratio of a spondee OO ('**whole** **world**') is 1, of an iamb oO ('be **glad**') it is 2, and of a dactyl it is 3 Ooo '**Cur**eton').

Part 1

# The poetic gestalt

# 1

# Verse systems and principles of rhythm

## Principles of rhythm

Lately, studies in prosody have succeeded in distinguishing the separate versification systems of different cultures and epochs. Most important here is the work of Mihail Gasparov. He has established the main systems, like French syllabic versification or Chinese syllabomelodic versification (see Introduction, p. 6; Gasparov 1996: 3–4). A *versification system* relies on a certain *rhythmical principle* with the addition of some sets of rules.

I will distinguish three different rhythmical principles, hereby following Richard Cureton's three so-called temporalities in poetry: tactus, grouping and prolongation (Cureton 1992: 126–53). In accordance with Cureton's division, I will classify aesthetic rhythm after three principles: serial rhythm, sequential rhythm, and dynamic rhythm, which are three basic sets of gestalt qualities (Hopsch and Lilja 2007: 364).

- *Serial rhythm*: Tactus or beat in measured music and poetry. A pale fence is also serial like the colonnades of an antique temple.
- *Sequential rhythm*: The sequence of a phrase, which is to be found in free verse and in Old Greek poetry, in the half line of the four-beat medieval line, in music and in the surface of a painting, as well as in the parts of a sculpture or a piece of architecture.
- *Dynamic rhythm*: The forces and directions in two- and three-dimensional artefacts, and the temporal intensification towards a focus in music and poetry; that is, the semantic rhythm of a prolongation.

There are differences in extent between them. One tactus in music or poetry covers about half a second. This time span signifies the iamb, a very common kind of tactus, but also a walking step. A sequence takes a couple of seconds and covers a phrase or a verse line. Carmen's legs and arms, in the picture below, create sequences in the dynamic play between parts of a wholeness. However, temporal art forms also work with dynamic rhythm. In a poem, it could be about prolongations, or semantic tensions between stanzas, and in music the intensification towards a focus (Kühl 2003; 2007).

The three principles of rhythm make three kinds of gestalts when forming the rhythm of a free-verse poem: sequences, dynamics, and tactus. A piece of art mostly uses them all to varying degrees, or at least two of them. However, painting, sculpture, and architecture start out of dynamic rhythms, while temporal art forms, like poetry and music, proceed from sequences and seriality (Ellestrøm 2010b: 19). Dynamic rhythm has its base in the whole dynamic form, when sequential and serial rhythm begin with the short segment.

So, the three kinds of rhythm mix in most pieces of art, even if one of them is usually the primary one. Older prosody were, in the first place, interested in

**Figure 1.1** Carmen's dance forms sequences in a dynamic play. However, ballroom dancing follows the serial principle. Seriality overruns the now and the gestalt might go on forever, as all devoted dancers know. Photo © Nobu Yamamoto.

seriality, partly because this was the common verse principle before modernism and partly due to the fascinating qualities of metre. Tactus has a capability to hypnotize readers – anybody could lose their mind in the flow of regular beats. For shamans, tactus has been a method of getting closer to God and, for my generation, Elvis Presley's music had something of the same effect. A series of pairs makes a very strong gestalt. However, this book investigates the rhythms of free verse.

When looking back at verse history, the rhythmical principle of measured poetical forms from the Renaissance up to Romanticism is serial. But serial rows would hardly manage without the embracing of rhythmic sequence. The rhythmical principle of Germanic medieval accentual versification, as well as of modernist free verse, is basically sequential. Medieval poets, as well as modernist ones, used structured sequences in combination with a powerful segmentation when shaping poetry. However, the old and the new style differ regarding their sets of rules, respectively. Or, modern poetry repudiates any rule of versification.

In verse history, there is a long period of fading seriality and an increasing knowledge about how to handle rhythmic sequences artistically. Eliot's poems might illustrate this transition period. They exemplify a beautiful cooperation between serial and sequential rhythms (cf. Ch. 7).

## Versification systems

Poetry is a global phenomenon, but ages and places have constructed it in various ways. Technical possibilities are decided from the actual language – how it notes the relationship between strong and weak elements, how it builds its patterns. Old Greek poetry used pronunciation spans, long or short syllables, while the French alexandrine worked with phrase accents, and German poems with distinct stresses. Then a rhythmical principle – serial, sequential or dynamic – was added, together with local conventions. In this way, the different versification systems evolved.[1]

Ancient Greek quantitative metre can scarcely be adapted to literatures in northern Europe. However, many unhappy attempts have been made. The lovely

---

[1] A map of the European versification systems is to be seen in Gasparov 1996: xviii. For a shorter version, which also takes free verse into account, see Lilja 2006: 182.

ancient measures attracted the poets with results that became inspiring as well as devastating. Through time, the Germanic cultures have had their own varieties, but English and German hexameter does not sound like the Athenian hexameter.

In English poetry and Germanic literature, one should take into account at least four versification systems as follows:

- Accentual versification of the three- or four-beat line in the Middle Ages.
- The tactus of accent-syllabic poetry.
- French syllabic verse.
- The free versification of Modernist poetry.

Accentual verse counts the number of stresses of a line but does not care about the weak elements. In practice, an accentual verse line is a stylized speech phrase, often built out of two phrases of two stresses each. Two such lines keep together with the help of some rhyme. The formula could be $2 \times (2 + 2)$. Lovely examples of this form are to be found in Old Norse poetry, in *Beowulf* and in German poetry, in the *Hildebrandslied* fragments (Gasparov 1996: 36). Accentual versification remained in popular forms when high-brow poems became cadenced. Ballads, nursery rhymes, and working songs used accentual verse; mostly the irregular four-beat line (Lilja 2006: 203; Attridge 2013: 147–49; Attridge 2012).

Tactus, or metre, developed slowly in northern Europe out of the influence of music. Most poems at that time were performed with music and had the limiting force of the French eight-syllable line (Wagenknecht 1971: 40, 72–3). The correct handling of the tactus took some time, and the development period lasted probably from the ninth to the seventeenth centuries. However, through time, unregulated weak syllables gave a barbaric impression. In this respect, the countries of northern Europe displayed varying movements.[2] When the tactus was at last introduced, this pattern proved to be very strong, and difficult to get rid of later on. It often hammers somewhere on the bottom of modern poetic language.

The period of tactus lasts approximately from the Renaissance through Romanticism – just a few centuries. However, England has its own story

---

[2] The oldest attempts took place with Otfried in southern Germany. The Scandinavian countries were the last to accept metered poetry, probably due to the high quality of their accentual verse forms. There was really no need for new rhythms.

concerning tactus in poetry (compare the Introduction, p. 8). When French syllabism appeared in England after 1066, forms changed. The French syllabic verse is really sequential in character and counts the number of syllables per phrase to get a uniform span; phrases that are structured with one accent that arrives at its very end (the standard French measure is the alexandrine with a basic pattern of 6 + 6 syllables in a line). Within this frame, the lengths of syllables vary somewhat untidily. These qualities constitute lovely French rhythms that have charmed the rest of Europe, but its basic pattern changes considerably in the encounter with the accent systems of other languages. For example, a Swedish alexandrine sounds rather stiff.

English pentameter has been much discussed. It is a fantastic measure, pliant and flexible. It works because it combines two verse systems, French syllabic verse and English disyllabic metre. Margaret Freeman explains this beautifully:

> I see English metre as the child of two parents in Indo-European tradition: Romance (of which French syllabics is one example) and Germanic (the stress-timed metres of Old English poetry). Blending helps me express English metre as emergent structure. Just as a child has features from both parents and their lineage, the child nevertheless is unique in its own right, with emergent structure that is different from either parent. It is that emergent structure that I think English metrists in the past have been trying to account for.
> 
> (Personal communication, 6 July 2014)

In the English pentameter, an iambic tactus cooperates with salient phrase rhythms. In practice, the pentameter line gets its finish with the help of another verse system, the older four-beat line. A pentameter line is mostly divided by a caesura with two realized prominences on each part. The result comes close to the medieval accentual verse system. The seemingly irregular English pentameter is a historical phenomenon that is best understood considering the English history of language.[3]

Modernist free verse largely uses the sequential rhythmic principle, just like the medieval forms. However, it acknowledges no rules, which is something that has made it inconvenient to handle within versification studies. A century has passed since its introduction, and an accurate investigation has still not taken place.

---

[3] Much of Reuven Tsur's work attempts to explain what happens in the meeting between the at least two verse systems in English iambic pentameter. See, for example, Tsur 2012a. Also compare with Attridge 1982.

The Introduction shows how the diverse origins of free versification also initiated different rhythm patterns (pp. 7–8). One tradition has developed forms from Old Greek poetry, such as enjambments, spondees OO, and molossi OOO. Another tradition has taken as its base the medieval four-beat line where speech rhythm is sharpened to salient phrases. In addition, a tradition of long-liners varies the streaming syllables of Psaltar translations. However, the models are treated in opposition to their old protocols – the verse must be free, as one can understand from the many manifestos of the various modernist movements.

There is a fourth tradition, starting from the Dada performances at Cabaret Voltaire in Zürich 1916. The true start of the European avant-garde happened here, including, among other things, a workshop for experiments in the auditive and visual possibilities of poetry. During the course of the twentieth century, the wild tradition of Dada has often remained in the dark. However, it reached a high point in the 1950s when German and Scandinavian poets developed Concretism, and Isidore Isou in Paris launched Lettrism. Lately, conceptual poetry has continued these experiments, now also with the help of digital tools.

As to versification, Marjorie Perloff takes the position that this avant-garde poetry should not be regarded as free verse. This is because the very defining device of verse is sometimes missing here; namely lineation – the division of the text in short lines. She then has to redefine versification in light of avant-garde poetry by speaking about a subtly formed language (Perloff 1999).

## Plath's 'Winter Trees'

Sylvia Plath's 'Winter Trees' will represent the rhythmic principles and a couple of versification systems.

|    |    | Line | Scansion |
|----|----|------|----------|
|    |    | The wet dawn inks are doing their blue dissolve. | o OOO / o O oo O o O |
| 2  |    | On their blotter of fog the trees | oo O oo O / o O> |
|    |    | Seem a botanical drawing – | O / oo O oo O o |
| 4  |    | Memories growing, ring on ring, | O oo O o / O o O |
|    |    | A series of weddings. | o O oo O o |
|    |    |      |          |
| 6  |    | Knowing neither abortions nor bitchery, | O o O oo O o / OO oo |
|    |    | Truer than women, | O oo O o |
| 8  |    | They seed so effortlessly! | o O o O o o |
|    |    | Tasting the winds, that are footless, | O oo O / oo O0 |
| 10 |    | Waist-deep in history – | OO / o O oo |

|     | Full of wings, otherworldliness. | O o **O** / O o **O** oo |
| --- | --- | --- |
| 12  | In this, they are Ledas. | o **O** / oo **O** o |
|     | O mother of leaves and sweetness | **OO** o / o **O** o **O** o |
| 14  | Who are these pietàs? | **OO** o **O** oo |
|     | The shadows of ringdoves chanting, | o **O** oo **OOO** o/o **O** o **O** o |
|     | but easing nothing. | |

(Sylvia Plath, 'Winter Trees', Collected Poems, 1981)

This poem compares the life of trees with the married life of women. The wedding occurs in the first stanza. In the second, conception takes place, and in the third, two mythical mothers meet in two aspects of motherhood. The winter of the first stanza turns into some kind of springtime in the second. At the beginning of the last stanza, there is a summer that fades away in the last lines. Winter possesses this poem, but summer disposes of a parallel mythical scene. The shadows in line 15 re-establish contact with the realistic landscape of the first lines, but, at the same time, they act like shadows of Hades.

According to the versification system, 'Winter Trees' mixes traditional characteristics of measured poetry with modernistic ones. Many lines could be read with mixed tactus where a trisyllabic metre hovers over the text (e.g. l. 2–5 or l. 12–13). The form of this poem plays with traditional measures, having stanzas with a regular number of lines and some kind of end rhyming – even if the rhymes mostly consist of assonances, like 'ring' (l. 4) – 'winds' (l. 9) – 'wings' (l. 11) – 'nothing' (l. 15).

However, the tactus is not allowed to take over. The most obvious breaks happen in line 8 and line 11, where dissyllabic rows do not cooperate with the dancing trisyllabics that might be heard in, for example, lines 4–5 and 12–14. The enjambment of line 2 is another spot where a possible tactus breaks down. This free verse has some traditional features, but it is still a part of the modernistic free-verse system.

Concerning principles of rhythm, analyses have shown that a poem mostly uses two or three principles of rhythm, and this is also the case here in Plath's 'Winter Trees'. Salient sequences (like l. 1:1 'The wet dawn inks' o **OOO**) are mixed with rows of serial elements (like l. 12 'In this, they are Ledas' o **O** oo **O** o). The repeated cretic **O**o**O** 'ring on ring' (l. 1 'blue dissolve', l. 2 'fog the trees') supports the alternating lines 8 and 11.[4] The serial rows and the sequential phrases have the same weight for the rhythmic impression of the poem. Moreover, many

---

[4] I will use the ancient Greek labels for phrase rhythms. A list is to be found at p. 31.

sequences here have an Old Greek touch like the adonii Ooo Oo of line 4 and line 7. Also, the enjambment of line 2 – extending the main word of this poem, 'trees'– is a classical device just like the falling ionic OO oo of line 6:2, 'nor bitchery', and the rising one in line 9:2, 'that are footless' oo O0.

The spatial rhythm of typography must, of course, be dynamic, as should the prolongations. 'Prolongation' means a direction towards the central point of information, the 'goal' – in the notation scheme above marked with bold rings. Weaker phrases are anticipating or extending the goal of a sentence. 'Anticipations' cause rising movements and 'extensions' bring falling movements (see Introduction, p. 6 and Cureton 1992: 146 and following). In 'Winter Trees', the lines are grouped in prolongations like this:

l. 1, 2–3, 4–5         goals: wet, trees, ring
l. 6–8, 9–10           goals: eff(ortlessly), winds
l. 11–12, 13–14, 15    goals: wings, moth(er), chant(ing)

The first and the last lines of the poem are closed and very long. They provide prolongations of their own. The beginning of stanza 2 constitutes an expansive prolongation of three lines.

The additions of rhythm and rhyme influence the interpretation of this poem. Furthermore, rhythm and significance cooperate. There are at least two rhythmical themes, as follows:

- A mixed serial rhythm most obviously expressed in the adonii O oo O o (l. 4, 7). However, the slow performance that is needed here prevents the tactus and underlines rhythmic details.[5] A serial rhythm is most evident in lines 2–5 and lines 12–13.
- The cretic OoO 'ring on ring' in 4:2, which is repeated in 11:1 'Full of wings', seems to be the centre of this poem as to rhythm as well as significance. Firstly, the cretic OoO of 4:2 'ring on ring' seems to collect the word music of this poem as well as the most important motives and themes of the poem. It is the centre of a series of significant assonances, ink – doing – drawing – growing – ring – wedding – knowing – tasting – winds – wings – ringdoves – chanting – easing – nothing. '[R]ing' is also a metaphor with many meanings – the ringing sound, marriage, wholeness,

---

[5] Susan Bassnett remarks that this poem should be read slowly (2005: 116). This calls for a reading style that strengthens possible prominences, like the molossi of l. 1 and l. 15 and the spondees of l. 6, 9, 10, 13, and 14.

the annual rings, and the rings of a water surface and so on. The sound pattern creates an impression of echoing (Bassnett 2005: 116).

The cretic is a strong gestalt with a penetrating power. Here it extends and doubles a couple of times to a dissyllabic tact; for example, in line 8 and the corresponding 11:2, as follows:

| | | |
|---|---|---|
| l. 8 | They seed so effortlessly! | o O o O o O o |
| l. 11 | Full of wings, otherworldliness. | O o O / O o O o O |

Line 8 depicts a moment of happy fertilization.[6] Possibly, line 11 complicates the happy moment of line 8 referring to the Leda myth. Dressed as a swan, Zeus seduced or raped Leda, the queen of Sparta, who gave birth to twins. The dissyllabics of line 13:2 '[O mother] of leaves and sweetness' repeat the rhythm of line 8, thus keeping the sweet summer for one moment more. However, the next repetition, in line 15:2, expresses despair by listening to the ringdoves from the kingdom of the dead ('shadows' mark the antique death). The extended cretics OoO in line 13:2 and line 15:2 underline the focus on line 8 and line 11 when closing the poem. They are both phrases in balance.

If the rooted trees in this poem stand for a kind of female principle, the male counterpart consists of birds, wings, and air. Two mythical figures may be found in the last stanza. Other than Leda, in art history 'pietà' denotes the Virgin Maria, another mother of a God, when mourning her dead son. Leda and Maria are both taken by Gods and give birth to extraordinary men with sad fates. Leda is here focused as a bride and Maria as a mourning mother. They parallel and are in contrast with each other. Conceptions could be better or worse. The state of being deep-rooted gives advantages that are not shared by the airy birds.

In this poem, the rather stable patterns relieve each other. The mixed serial rhythm covers most space, but the cretics OoO dominate emphatic passages. As in most poems, the sequential principle dominates – the sequence characterizes the poem with the addition of changing amounts of serial moments. This Plath poem has shown us the play between two rhythmic principles within the frame of the free-verse system.

---

[6] David Wood remarks that l. 8 'They seed so effortlessly!' 'constitutes a soothing moment in her troubled landscape'. The poem returns to grief, but the moment has had its value of solace, he says. (Wood 1992: 161.)

# 2

# The rhythmic gestalt

## The patterned line

The basic entity in versification is the line. A common line within all verse systems embraces roughly ten syllables taking about three seconds to read (Turner and Pöppel 1983). The time span of the short-term memory is approximately three seconds – the amount of time experienced as 'now', or the subjective present (Pöppel 2004). In this way, a physical fact coincides with a versification standard. Of course, there are much longer and much shorter verse lines than this standard of ten syllables, but then the reader will apprehend them as long or short.

Later on in this book (in Chapter 5), I will elaborate more on some of the consequences of this coincidence. For now, I will only emphasize the importance of the unity of a line. Speaking of rhythm, the line could be looked upon as a patterned moment. The sounds of the line are ordered according to models derived from various bodily functions (e.g. breathing, pulse, sex; see Chapter 8) or from culture and tradition (see Chapters 7 and 9). In this respect, the line behaves the same way as every other kind of information: it must be handled with a view to the conditions of the short-term memory, which perceives solar systems and seasons within the time frame of the three seconds. While it is true that the latter two phenomena in themselves exist on quite another scale, the four seasons of the year and the four syllables of a short phrase are both subject to approximately the same type of patterning: springtime – SUMMER – autumn – WINTER, which could be notated as oO oO – a double iamb. Different kinds of concepts are patterned according to the same gestalts according to the three-second limit.

A main theme here is that, in the reading process, rhythm emerges in the reader (or viewer or listener). This being the case, there is some kind of relationship between the individual and the artwork. The poem (or the picture or the piece of music) provides the impulses needed to order gestalts. Rhythm can thus be seen as order within a perceived poem's gestalt.

## The gestalt in versification

We can immediately observe that the whole poem is a gestalt; one to be heard but also seen. However, a poem offers many other gestalts, both big and small, such as phrases, lines and stanzas. Like a human body, the poem creates a hierarchy that ranges from the one big gestalt to many small phrases. The whole poem is caught in one single glance. The phrase, on the other hand, is heard but not so easily seen. Stanza and line, for their part, are easy to both look at and listen to.

As already noted in the Introduction, Reuven Tsur (2008) has drawn upon Gestalt psychology to work out a concept of gestalt suitable for use in versification studies.

> **Law of proximity** – In an assortment of objects, objects that are near to one another are seen as forming a group.
>
> **Law of similarity** – In an assortment of objects, objects that are similar to one another tend to be perceptually grouped together.
>
> **Law of closure** – Forms and figures such as shapes, letters, pictures, etc., are perceived as a complete whole even when they are not complete if they are close enough.
>
> **Law of continuity** – Elements of objects tend to be grouped together, and thus integrated into perceptual wholes, if they are aligned within it.
>
> **Law of good gestalt** – Elements of objects tend to be perceptually grouped together if they form a pattern that is regular, simple and orderly.

According to Tsur, the line in a poem makes up a unity – a system determining the character of its parts. Perceptions of the world are mainly apprehended as entireties (Ash 1995: 88; Tsur 2012a).

The Gestalt school of psychology emerged in Berlin and Frankfurt in the early years of the twentieth century. The general laws of how the human mind creates gestalts, or meaningful entireties, were first formulated by Max Wertheimer in 1923 (see, e.g., Ash 1995: 106). The basic observation here is that visual elements perceptually group according to how they, in some respect, hang together, because they have the same form, colour, direction, or the like. Cureton has termed these generalities as 'grouping principles', adapting them to the needs of versification (Cureton 1992: 190). Elements should be close enough, similar enough, or in some other respect sufficiently related to one another, with this relation then constituting the rhythm.

Behind these laws, the means of versification can be recognized. Rhymes of different kinds activate the law of similarity, while the proximity of syllables is necessary for an expressive patterning. The law of continuity makes it possible to pattern elements that are not so close to one another within a prolongation (see the Introduction, p. 6). At the same time, however, one also strives to create gestalts that are as good as possible. What does a 'good' shape refer to here? Most immediately, it refers to harmony and expressiveness, to regular patterns. In terms of versification, this probably means a great many repetitions of all kinds.

Of the gestalt laws above, it is perhaps the law of closure that is the most important. The border of the gestalt determines its shape. It must be closed, but in poetry one must await the reading process for closure. In a temporal gestalt, the reader strives for the limit closing the form in co-operation with what sound impulses make possible – such as a small pause, or a falling intonation curve in the phrase end. Old measures like the four-beat line, the hexameter, and the alexandrine regulate the pauses or caesuras in their rules.

Even experience will influence how to shape the gestalts – practice may stimulate a reader to prefer one certain gestalt or apprehend one gestalt but not another. Such experienced gestalts can explain why one knows when a piece of music is drawing to its end. Subtle acoustic signals indicate that closure is approaching (Arnheim 2004; Meyer 1956: 129). Completion needs a solid limit – the borderline of the gestalt.

Once a stable gestalt has been perceived, it will be difficult to change it, even if the sound structure allows other shapes to emerge. Such possibilities disappear once the reader has established his or her perceived form. In other words, in temporal gestalts, the form is grasped backwards. To borrow the term of Tsur (2012a: 302; see also Smith 1968), it is 'back-structured'. In the very moment of listening, impulses are waiting for a boundary, and the form's internal order emerges after the gestalt closes.

A salient form arises when a form meets the reader's perception process which prefers significant forms (or, in German, *Prägnanz*) – forms that are stipulated in the so-called 'gestalt laws of grouping'. This principle of *Prägnanz* is the lasting heritage of this old school of psychology, and it implies that perceptual phenomena will always be organized in a way that is the most simple and meaningful (Tsur 2008: 507).

## Phrases – Old and new

Turner and Pöppel demonstrated (1983) that an ordinary line uses approximately ten syllables according to the limit of the short-term memory. So does the standard intonation curve of an ordinary speech phrase. Spontaneously, one divides it in two parts – two smaller phrases of about two prominences each. Historically, these small phrases have turned out to be the very base of patterning verse. The first line of Anne Sexton's poem 'The Fury of Rain Storms' is cited below:

l. 1   The rain drums down like red ants,          o O o O / o OO

The line is a short one, only seven syllables, but it retains the basic model. There are at least two spectacular phrase patterns for free verse, the Old Norse versification in its medieval form and the colon system of ancient Greece. The Icelandic verse works with an ordinary speech phrase, making it salient with the help of alliterations and small significant stylizations. The Greek figures are more heavy and solemn.

In the Introduction, I distinguished between certain traditions of free verse based on how they were originally created. Heine's free versification was inspired by forms of medieval German lyrics, the four-beat line that represents the continuation of Old Norse verse forms. I also mentioned Attridge's achievements, paying attention to the medieval four-beat line. Its base is an intonation phrase made of two smaller phrases and a pause in the line break. Every half line has two beats, but the weak syllables in between may behave in whichever manner, which allows fluctuating line lengths. The rhythm may be bumpy; especially in older varieties. In the history of free verse, this basic pattern has been the most popular. Although free verse is indeed free – that is, it does not follow any rules – it still adapts to poetic modes.

The Greek poets created their verse patterns with the help of small rhythmic pieces – colons that were constructed of long and short syllables (see, e.g., Maas 1962; Raven [1962] 1998; West 1982). Klopstock loved antique phrases, and tried to transfer them to the accents of modern German. Here is a selection:

| | | | |
|---|---|---|---|
| oO | iamb | Oo | trochee |
| ooO | anapaest | Ooo | dactyl |
| OO | spondee | OOO | molossus |
| oOO | bacchius, rising | OOo | bacchius, falling |
| OoO | cretic | oOo | amfibrach |
| ooOO | ionic, rising | OOoo | ionic, falling |
| OooO | choriamb | oOOo | antispast |
| Oooo, oOoo, ooOo, oooO  paeon | | OOOo, OOoO, OoOO, oOOO  epitrite | |
| Ooo Oo | adonius | | |

I will use the Old Greek labels for rhythmic figures when describing the rhythms of a poem. While European versification studies mainly adopted four of them early on – iamb, trochee, anapaest and dactyl – there are many more expressive figures. The Greeks preferred those figures consisting of several long syllables; lengths that history has tried to transfer to Germanic prominences or stresses. Since the figures were so distinct, the ancient poets did not care much to denote line breaks, thus verse inspired by Greek forms often uses enjambments. The beginning of a line can be loose, but the endings are often very structured. The last line pair in Sexton's poem uses Greek forms:

l. 13    and I would do better to make        oooo O oo O >
       some soup and light up the cave.        OO / oOO oO

We recognize the weak beginning of line 13, as well as the enjambment and the two spondees in line 14. Moreover, the syllable stress ratio of line 14 is very low, only 1.4, meaning that most syllables are stresses, making the line slow and heavy. This is typical of ancient lyrical measures. Here, this heaviness is a way to close the poem (see pp. 13–14 for an explanation of the notation signs and the term 'syllable stress ratio').

The style here, however, is not very solemn. Despite its easy-going tone, the poem speaks of suicide, disintegration and death. The rhythm of a poem often reveals hidden themes that hint at interpretations other than the obvious ones.

## Anne Sexton, 'The Fury of Rain Storms'

I will now take a look at phrases and other gestalts in Anne Sexton's poem 'The Fury of Rain Storms', which is part of a suite entitled 'The Furies' (first printed in Sexton's 1974 collection *The Death Notebooks*). This poem, about bad weather, succeeds in jumping between red ants and wet graves, it is ironic and grotesque, and it uses rhythm very skilfully to shape a number of different emotions.

|    | The rain drums down like red ants,     | o OOO o OO              |
|----|----------------------------------------|-------------------------|
| 2  | each bouncing off my window.           | OO o O o O o            |
|    | These ants are in great pain           | OO oo OO                |
| 4  | and they cry out as they hit,          | oo OO oo O              |
|    | as if their little legs were only      | o O ooo O o O o >       |
| 6  | stitched on and their heads pasted.    | OO / oo OO o            |
|    | And oh they bring to mind the grave,   | o O / o O o O o O       |
| 8  | so humble, so willing to be beat upon  | o O o / o O o oo O o O  |
|    | with its awful lettering and           | oo O o O oo O >         |
| 10 | the body lying underneath              | o O o O ooo O           |
|    | without an umbrella.                   | o O oo O o              |
| 12 | Depression is boring, I think,         | o O oo O o / o O        |
|    | and I would do better to make          | o 0 oo O oo O >         |
| 14 | some soup and light up the cave.       | OO / oOO oO             |

(Anne Sexton, 'The Fury of Rain Storms', *The Death Notebooks*, 1974)

Some rules of thumb for reading free verse are discussed in the Introduction (pp. 11–12). When investigating the sound system in order to fully experience the poem, one will have to twist every stress when listening to its signification. Subconsciously, however, the reader may have taken it all in already – versification studies may bring an intuition to the surface, feeble impressions that the analyses will then justify (Tsur 2012b: 194).

Sexton's poem above consists of 14 lines, just like an English sonnet. The lines here are roughly the same length, ranging between six and nine syllables and, counting the number of stresses, mainly between three and four. There is a *volta* – the sonnet's change of theme, but not in the ordinary place after line 8 or 12, but as soon as after line 6, where the ants leave the poem and the grave enters the scene. This is a reversed sonnet with 6+8 lines.

Above, I noted how the last line – along with the first – has a very low syllable stress ratio. On p. 14, I explained this tool that gives the relationship between strong and weak parts of a line, the same value as metered verse captures with the difference between an iamb oO (SSR 2) and an anapaest (SSR 3). Figure 2.1 shows how this rate is calculated for every line of the Sexton poem above. The number of syllables is divided by the number of stresses, giving the syllable stress ratio. For example, line 1 needs 7 syllables, where 5 are stresses. The division gives a syllable stress ratio (SSR) of 1.4.

| Line | Syllables | Stresses | SSR |
| --- | --- | --- | --- |
| 1 | 7 | 5 | 1.4 |
| 2 | 7 | 4 | 1.7 |
| 3 | 6 | 4 | 1.5 |
| 4 | 7 | 3 | 2.3 |
| 5 | 9 | 3 | 3.0 |
| 6 | 7 | 4 | 1.7 |
| 7 | 8 | 4 | 2.0 |
| 8 | 11 | 4 | 2.8 |
| 9 | 8 | 3 | 2.7 |
| 10 | 8 | 3 | 2.7 |
| 11 | 6 | 2 | 3.0 |
| 12 | 8 | 3 | 2.7 |
| 13 | 8 | 3 | 2.7 |
| 14 | 7 | 5 | 1.4 |

**Figure 2.1** Line lengths and SSR for 'The Fury of Rain Storms'.

As already noted, ordinary speech mostly uses a stress ratio between 2 and 3, which corresponds to about one or two weaks per stress. Many lines in 'The Fury of Rain Storms' exhibit that relationship, although some ratios are lower – in lines 1 to 3, 6 and 14. These lines have more strong stresses than weak, which goes against the habits of common speech and creates severity in a kind of poetic mode.

In Sexton's poem, four parts could be distinguished, marked by the four complete sentences. There is an introductory line pair (l. 1–2), the ant part (l. 3–6), the grave part (l. 7–11) and the closing terza rima of depression (l. 12–14). I will now look at them a little more closely, one by one.

*The introductory line pair* (l. 1–2) is very heavy, with the two spondees OO and one molossus OOO, marking that the poem will now go into something important. I have already pointed at the low syllable stress ratio here – below 2 for three lines in a row. Walking through the poem, there is an obvious change from heaviness into rapid forward movement.

*The ant part* (l. 3–6) is also heavy in the beginning and at the end, given all its slow spondees, but here the ants are too small to carry that weight, producing an icy irony. Moreover, these ants bear all the signs of the grotesque and fall apart without any encouragement. Owing to the heaviness of the four spondees, lines 3 and 6 stand still, but the embraced lines of 4 and 5 start a strong forward movement, opening with an ionic ooOO plus an anapaest ooO, and continuing in the next line with four possible iambs oO – the first one in a series of iambic lines with a strong forward motion. Here the tempo increases to a rush, but the movement ends up with an enjambment that takes it over to line 6, where it disappears and encounters the full-stop spondee 'stitched on' OO.

While line 1 says that the ants are metaphors for the rain, in line 3 they have grown very vivid and are maltreated. In the next line, line 4, they even cry, but then lines 5 and 6 tell us that the ants are artificial and could not cry even if they were not metaphoric. This is then nothing but a creepy joke not worthy of spondaic importance or rushing panic in the rhythm. I would say that the rhythm supports the subtext when it uses different means of a strong expression to describe some ant toys. Something is rather spooky below the surface.

*The grave part* (l. 7–11) shifts the attention gently away from the ants towards the grave; both of them 'humble' and 'willing to be beat upon'. There is a contrast between the many spondees of the ant part and the iambs and anapaests of the grave part. These two figures are the quickest ones: due to gestalt behaviour, the weak parts of these figures shrink and the prominent parts grow (cf. Tsur 2017: 219). Their falling counterparts – trochee and dactyl – react in the opposite way, with their weak parts being extended while the prominent parts are contracted. How come the little ants are accorded the solemnity of many spondees while the serious grave rushes?

Line 7 is then the second iambic line and introduces a wet grave in a most hilarious voice, with the unnecessary 'oh' bringing about a marching tactus:

l. 7    And oh they bring to mind the grave,          o O / o O o O o O

Here the style and the rhythm sound happy next to the gloomy content. This is another ironic turn. In line 10, the iambic rhythm returns for the last time in a somewhat weakened form. The anapaests in line 9 support the iambs, and another enjambment increases the tempo. I read the enjambment with extra weight on the last syllable possible to stress, because it replaces the line break pause:

l. 9    with its awful lettering and                oo O o O oo / O>

However, the grave part is also closed in balance (l. 11) with two amphibrachs, repeating the two amphibrachs from line 8:

l. 8    so humble, so willing                      oOo / oOo
        ...
l. 11   without an umbrella.                       o O oo O o

The rhythm of line 11 is calm and balanced, delivering a bad joke – the dead bodies have no umbrella when it is raining. The grave part has an opposite problem compared with the preceding lines about screaming ants. Here the rhythm is too easy-going in telling us about the gruesome grave. Jolly iambs and anapaests alternate with calmer amphibrachs oOo. The forward direction is obvious, and the tempo increases. At first sight this rhythm seems to be misconstrued. It is too quick and joyful for the frightening grave.

First of all, the rhythm appears to support style, which is carefree, joking and easy-going. The style and the rhythm together create a distance which attempts to diminish the threatening death. I would say that it is precisely thanks to this distance that our uneasiness increases. The effort to reduce death only makes it grow stronger in the reader's imagination. The two layers of the text – the joking voice on the surface and the horror of the subtext – are significant for irony. (See Chapter 5 for more on irony and rhythm.)

In the grave part, iambs, anapaests and amphibrachs dominate the rhythm. The tempo increases, with the direction firmly pointing forward – to death, maybe. Above, I described such devices as joyful when viewed in combination with the style but, when applying the same rhythms to the gloomy content instead, other qualities are revealed – here there is too much of a hurry. The iambs hammer in panic when rushing towards the end.

*The terza rima of depression* (l. 12–14) completes the poem. The word 'depression' that begins at line 12 relates here to at least two things: bad weather and mental illness. The last three lines are about rain as well as illness, and they are evidently ambiguous. One text layer uses 'depression' for rainstorm, while another one deploys it to hint at a threatening suicide. A rainstorm will be more endurable with the help of 'some soup' (l. 14), while mental illness will not – here the irony returns and is stable (Booth 1974: 1). These lines use the same device of duality as the grave part – if read as a rainstorm, the depression means soup and candlelight, if it is read as illness, then it means deadly fear.

Also, the rhythm is both happy and panic-stricken at the same time. This implies quick movements – the body moves easily in both situations, a fact that Sexton has utilized here (cf. Tsur 2012b: 142, 146). The rhythm can be adapted to both meanings – a happy rush or panic. It is a small rhythmical difference between the two interpretations. I suggest that in the panic version, the text will be read somewhat faster.

There is an ambiguity in lines 11 to 12. They can be read as anapaests as well as amphibrachs:

| l. 11 | without an umbrella. | oOo oOo *or* oO ooO o |
| l. 12 | Depression is boring, I think, | oOo oOo / oO *or* oO ooO ooO |

I interpret line 11 as amphibrachs oOo and line 12 as anapaests ooO because the weak (o) and determined closure (period) of line 11 hinders a rapid tempo and fortifies the softer amphibrachs. The following line 12 has a catchy iamb oO at the very end of the line, encouraging a strict forward movement read in anapaests ooO.

Both lines 12 and 13 quickly move forward, but in different ways. The anapaests of line 12 are vivid spoken language, but line 13 is really a catapult, especially if read as follows:

| l. 13 | and I would do better to make | oooo O oo O > | SSR 4 |

It rushes ahead towards the finishing enjambment and the spondee OO of the next line ('some soup'). Something very quick and light suddenly switches register, showing itself to be very dark and heavy instead. Lines 5 and 6 have prepared us for the concluding line pair of 13 and 14, with the first line of the pair running swiftly and jumping over into the spondee of the following line. The repeated rhythm helps to keep the poem together.

The very last line closes the poem, returning to the heavy syllable stress ratio (SSR) of the first line. Here, the irony is made very evident: 'and I would do better to', states line 13, as all the while the reader knows that there will be neither soup nor lit candles. 'Cave' (rhyming with 'grave') is then the word that collects all the threads and layers of the poem together. The 'I' is caught in a dark cave for good.

## Closure

This chapter has discussed gestalts in poems. Perceptual forces or tensions keep the line together as a whole (Tsur 2012a: 83, 86), simplifying the form into a 'good' gestalt. The figure must be closed before patterning in temporal gestalts, as these are back-structured. Line 12 exemplifies how a concluding iamb also may change the pattern at the beginning of the line:

| l. 12 | Depression is boring, I think, | oOo oOo / oO *or* oO ooO ooO |

The unity of the line is of primary importance. But there is a complication: the enjambment (cf. Ch. 10). Sexton's poem uses enjambment three times – in lines 5, 9 and 13. Here the phrase jumps over the line break, and the lines are not properly closed. The reader can proceed in different ways. One possibility is to pretend that there is no line break and just move on to the next line. Another is to make a full stop between, for example, 'only' (l. 5) and 'stitched' (l. 6). I prefer something in between, so as to lengthen the last syllable that can be stressed in the first line of the pair. Here the first syllable of 'only' Oo will then be given added prominence. In line 9, 'and' – surprisingly – will be given full stress because of its position, thereby preparing the reader for the introduction of the corpse. Line 13, however, is even more complicated. Its last syllable 'make' should be prominent anyhow, but here it goes, together with the following spondee in line 14, into a kind of molossus OOO. With no enjambment, 'make some soup' would probably invite a differentiated reading, such as OoO or OoO. Now all three syllables will have full stress (cf. Kjørup 2008), with the 'soup' being elevated to something very important.

I have referred above to a couple of ancient models for patterning gestalts: Old Greek colons and medieval lyrics. The Greeks preferred many long syllables, enjambments and low ratios, whereas the Germanic style patterned ordinary speech phrases into two short phrases of mostly two stresses each. Although free verse does not follow any rules, Greek and Norse styles can be recognized beneath the usual patterning in modernist verse. In fact, Sexton's poem exemplifies both of these styles, the Greek enjambments and low SSRs, and the two short phrases of the Germanic style.

Greek style:

| | | |
|---|---|---|
| l. 1 | The rain drums down like red ants, | o OoO o OO |
| l. 3 | These ants are in great pain | OO oo OO |
| l. 5 | as if their little legs were only | ooo o o O o O o > |
| l. 6 | stitched on and their heads pasted. | OO / oo OO o |
| l. 14 | some soup and light up the cave. | OO / oOO oO |

Germanic medieval style:

| | | |
|---|---|---|
| l. 8 | so humble, so willing to be beat upon | o O o o O o / oo O o O |
| l. 9 | with its awful lettering and | O o O o O oo / O |
| l. 10 | the body lying underneath | o O o O o / o o O |

Sexton's poem blends emphasis with quick tempo in a forward direction. There is an easiness as well as an affirmation. The rapidly directed lines follow the gestalt law of continuity. At the same time, the law of similarity is just as important. All the spondees at the beginning of the poem, for example, repeat and recall one another. I have already noted how the rhyming effect of the amphibrachs in line 8 is repeated in line 11. These echoing rings penetrate the entire poem even if there are no end rhymes.

Tsur has convincingly shown how similarity feeds back (Tsur 2012a: 303). This is also a main theme in Roman Jakobson's reflections about poetics. His so-called principle of equivalence emphasizes all kinds of similarities in poems, even if rhyme remained crucial for him (Jakobson 1960: 358). Evidently, the second rhyme word keeps the first one alive in the reading mind. While Jakobson never spells out why this would be so, back-structuring explains how this might happen. In keeping with the law of similarity, the second rhyme word creates gestalt closure. An end-rhymed line pair makes a closed gestalt. In Sexton's poem, the equivalences at first hand consist of rhythmic repetitions, but they still function to keep the gestalts closed.

# 3

# Rhythm and significance

## The signification of materiality

A work of art always signifies something (Lilja 2006: 123; Tsur 2012b: 1). Significance is the very purpose of all kinds of art (Johnson 2018: 25; Madsen 1990: 32–33; Rohrer 2005: 165, 173). All elements in an art work take part in this signification process, when more hidden ways of producing significance complement lexical meaning.[1]

The sounds and images of a poem signify in other ways than the pure lexical meaning. These kinds of significance are rather vague even if the form may be distinct.[2] When thinking of music, this circumstance shows up more evidently. The sound in music delivers joy and suffering in its own way with the help of rhythms and timbres. However, in some way different listeners mostly agree on its expression. The form in music is distinct but the significance is more undetermined.

The significance of pure sound is mainly about feeling and attitude. However, what rhythm stresses will also be emphasized in interpretation, and, of course, even the opposite is true – weak form elements suit less important messages (Tynyanov [1924] 1981: 82–83). The significance of sound elements are concerned with emotion (Starr 2013: 33). The sensuous parts of language add mood and timbre to semantic meaning. Pauses, directions and stresses evoke feeling – to be understood immediately and subconsciously.[3] Dynamic, balance, tempo, direction, stability and the like add significance as they allude to the reader's experiences.

This does not mean that the lexical reference of a word will diminish other than in a relative manner. The signification of sounds is about stronger and

---

[1] Poetry has two levels of perception: the semiotic text and the phenomenological process of the author and the reader (Freeman 2009: 185). Objects are understood by a subject who is not able to grasp them completely. Understanding takes place according to semiotic categories.
[2] Tsur gives an account of the interaction between the left and the right halves of the brain when reading poetry (e.g. Tsur 2017: 44).
[3] Sensation and emotion produce feeling. Meaning is embodied in the sound structure (Freeman 2009: 175).

weaker, emphasized and held back, volatile and blunt, quick and slow, far away and close, embodied memories, associations and even more subtleties. However, together their impact on the interpretation influences meaning to a great extent. Mostly, they strengthen as well as variegate the literal meaning, but sometimes there is a conflict between sound and semantics. For example, sayings about peace could be executed in noisy sounds and bumpy rhythms.

In such cases, the sound layer should be the trustworthy part of the dictum. The rhythm might speak for itself besides the semantic meaning as in line 11 in Heaney's 'Night Drive' (the whole poem is cited below):

l. 11   A forest fire smouldered out.        o O o O o / O o O

A forest fire should be vivid and wild but here the rhythm is balanced and quiet. So, one understands that this fire wasn't that bad. Yes, it smouldered out.

Talking about *gesture*, communication is added as an aspect of the gestalt. The gesture is to be apprehended as an act of signification. It is part of a communication between producer and recipient – it says something (Merleau-Ponty [1945] 2002: 226). And, as mentioned above, a piece of art always signifies. This is because by definition art signifies – signification is the purpose of art. The gesture might be defined as a gestalt with signification, or, in other words, in art a limited movement is a gestalt, which is a gesture.

A gesture can signify emotional qualities like rest and energy, rapidity, emphasis and forward direction. All these things are also aspects of rhythm. Progression as well as stress relate to apprehended direction – this observation is relevant for visual arts as well as for poetry and music (Stougaard Pedersen 2008: 103–4). Wassily Kandinsky elaborated a theory for gestures or signs on a plane (Kandinsky [1928] 1955: 131–5). In his paintings, the shapes on the canvas are looked upon as gestures; expressions of freedom and imprisonment, safety and creativity.

A gestalt is a compact whole – a small one as well as a big one. Once you have apprehended the form, it will be almost impossible to change your view of it. Perceptions bring to the fore some accessible patterns in order to interpret the sound impulses, but long-term memory is not able to keep many patterns alive at the same time (Kühl 2003: 95). This makes the reader most sensitive to the present pattern, but insusceptible to impulses that may lead to other patterns.[4]

---

[4] This phenomenon explains why metered poetry can diverge significantly from the rule without losing the feeling of tactus, which is something that Reuven Tsur has investigated closely (Tsur 2012a).

# Rhythm and Significance

**Figure 3.1** Wassily Kandinsky, 'Composition 8', 1923. © 2022. The Solomon R. Guggenheim Foundation/Art Resource, NY/ Scala, Florence.

Seamus Heaney's poem 'Night Drive' (below) will demonstrate some possibilities for sounds to make significance, to come from rhythm to happiness, and from pause to stability. The first possibility is about culture, which is an aspect that will be further addressed in Chapter 9. The reader recognizes different forms and their implications from the literary tradition; I will return to this later when reading a modern sonnet.

In addition, the poetic text lodges a bundle of opaque similarities. This phenomenon is called iconicity, and it has been thoroughly investigated lately (Nänny 2001; Ellström 2010a, 2017; Freeman 2017, 2020). In its most obvious case, the materiality of a poem imitates something in the world – a train bumping over the rails, for example, or the whisper of a wind. The rhythm of the poem may also relate to the biorhythms; imitating rhythms of the human body (they will be more closely investigated in Chapter 8). A poem may jump as well as rest, things that work in the poem below.

|   |   |   | Stresses |
|---|---|---|---|
|   | The smells of ordinariness | o O o O o 0 oo | 3 (4) |
| 2 | Were new on the night drive through France: | o O / oo OO o O | 4 |
|   | Rain and hay and woods on the air | O o O / o O oo O | 4 |
| 4 | Made warm draughts in the open car. | 0OO / oo O o O | 4 (5) |

|    | Signposts whitened relentlessly.              | OOO o / o O oo      | 4    |
|----|-----------------------------------------------|---------------------|------|
| 6  | Montreuil, Abbeville, Beauvais                | o O / oo O / o O >  | 3    |
|    | Were promised, promised, came and went,       | o O o / O o / O o O | 4    |
| 8  | Each place granting its name's fulfilment.    | OOO o / o O o O o   | 5    |
|    |                                               |                     |      |
|    | A combine groaning its way late               | oo OO o / o OO      | 4    |
| 10 | Bled seeds across its work-light.             | oO / o O o OO       | 4(5) |
|    | A forest fire smouldered out.                 | o O o O o / O o O   | 4    |
| 12 | One by one cafés shut.                        | O o O / o OO        | 4    |
|    |                                               |                     |      |
|    | I thought of you continuously                 | o O oo / o O o o o  | 3(4) |
| 14 | A thousand miles south where Italy            | o O o OO / o O oo > | 4    |
|    | Laid its loin to France on the darkened sphere. | O o O o O / oo O o O | 5(4) |
| 16 | Your ordinariness was renewed there.          | OO o O oo / oo OO   | 4(5) |

(Seamus Heaney, 'Night Drive', *Door into Dark*, 1969)

The versification builds on a four-line stanza. At the phrase level, there is some variation between a weak tactus and expressive sequences. Most of the tactus lines alternate (1, 7, 10, 11 and 13), but a couple of them are mixed (3 and 15). However, there are also more complicated rhythmic figures:

l. 4  oOO / oo O o O          Made warm draughts in the open car

or

l. 8  OOO o / o O o O o       Each place granting its name's fulfilment.

## Convention

I have already pointed at some techniques where form devices add significance to a poem. One important way is the field of scholarly conventions. A Petrarchan sonnet makes the reader think of love – tradition has produced this signification. The hexameter was used to show us heroes and their deeds, and the iambic pentameter became the measure of clear thoughts. The haiku should deliver an impression from nature, and so on.

The traditional stanza form dominates in Heaney's poem. In 'Night Drive', the lines are mostly of the same length – this classical line of eight syllables was inherited from French medieval poetry, but the four-beat lines of the medieval English four-line stanza are also at stake here. Almost every line in this poem can be read with four stresses, and sometimes it plays with the caesura of the four-beat rule, as is the case in lines 11 to 12:

| l. 11 | A forest fire smouldered out. | o O o O o / O o O | 4 |
|       | One by one cafés shut. | O o O / o OO | 4 |

Line 11 consists of four most regular iambs, but the following, line 12, is made of one cretic OoO and one bacchius oOO.

In the last stanza, lines are a bit longer, 9-9-10-10 syllables, which is closer to the so-called normal length of the English pentameter (Turner and Pöppel 1983; see above p. 27). Here comes the highlight of the poem, and the lengthening of the lines constructs the rhythmic closure together with a completing spondee, 'was renewed there' oo OO.

The medieval four-liner has never disappeared – it continues to live, among other genres, in songs and birthday rhyming (Attridge 1982) and as a covered pattern in very many poetic forms. Here, the stanza form and the, mostly, four beats of a line add closeness and confidence to the poem. In Northern Europe, readers are familiar with this four-liner from childhood. The somewhat bumpy alternation of many lines works in the same way.

## Iconicity

Iconicity is another way to produce significance. Rhythms and sounds might be similar to something in the world. The classical example here is the whispering wind that is coloured with the help of many 'sss'. Some poems lack lexical meaning, like children's tirades, medieval incantations, Dada poems and today's poems in so-called language materialism where articulation alone makes signification. Nonetheless, one can understand these texts. Some words are onomatopoeic; they seem to imitate the sound of trains and dogs and the susurrating willows. There is some kind of resemblance or isomorphism between form and significance (e.g. Plato 1939; Schrott 2011: 229–38).

Heaney's poem travels from Normandy to northern Italy and, among other things, its rhythm describes forwardness and driving. The iambic rows (l. 7, 11 and 13) work in this direction – they suit a narrative of moving forward (Tsur 2011).

| l. 7 | Were promised, promised, came and went, | o O o / O o / O o O |

The reader of a poem seems to be more than willing to find similarities between language and meaning. However, there are also such concrete resemblances. There is a metallic quality in a 'g', something to be explained by the acoustic pattern of a 'g' – partly the same pattern as when listening to a flick on a metal disc (Tsur 1992: 15). An 'r' communicates force because that sound will need some effort to be pronounced (Tsur 1992: 148). The opposite concerns a short 'i', that is easy to say and often used for small objects (Jakobson and Waugh 1979: 183–7).

Whispering has often been expressed with the help of an 's', and this habit has a reason – the 's' will not be suppressed when changing one's voice to a whisper. The vowels may disappear, but the 's' stays just as distinct (Hrushovski 1980). Also, experience may explain why one ascribes certain significance to some phonemes. The 's', for example, could be understood in different ways depending on the context (Tsur 2012b). It might remind us of whispering willows or the hush of a grim teacher.

Heaney's poem describes travelling, the happy continuing of the car as well as some bumpiness. Line 3 pictures a steady going-on, and l. 4 makes an extra shade with the introducing molossus:

| Rain and hay and woods on the air | O o O / o O oo O |
| l. 4  Made warm draughts in the open car. | 0OO / oo O o O |

The car moves on alright (l. 3), and the warm breeze in the face heightens the well-being of travelling (l. 4).

Of late, the phenomenon of iconicity in literature has been much discussed. The concept originates from Peircean semiotics, where it is divided into three subgroups: image, diagram and metaphor; three degrees of resemblance between sign and world (Nöth 2001). In the 1990s, Max Nänny started a series of conferences that changed and enlarged iconicity studies (e.g. Nänny 1986; Hancil and Hirst 2013). Among other things, he investigated how lineation, the line breaks, influence understanding – this is especially valuable knowledge for free versification studies (Nänny 2001). Margaret Freeman has constructed a concept of iconicity out of its subgroup metaphor, which includes blending (Freeman 2009: 169–96; 2008: 358; 2017, 2020). With the help of these tools she intends to grip the precategorial information of the poem in order to explain why the experience of a poem can be so pervasive (Freeman 2020; Tsur 2012b: 12–13). Iconicity is the means by which poetry creates the semblance of felt life. A poem is an icon of reality, she says, and defines iconicity as the mechanism by which forms of feeling are represented in language, which create sensations, emotions and images that are apprehended as real (Freeman 2009: 170, 177; 2020).

In versification studies, another sub-group of iconicity is more interesting; namely the diagrammatic icon that implicates some kind of structural resemblance or isomorphism between sensorimotor impulses and something in the reader's conception of the world. Thoughts and feelings picture the world and have form as well (Hanslick [1854] 1955; Tsur 2012b: 140). As a matter of fact, thinking and feeling are spatial in nature, according to neurology as well as the field of rhetoric (Lakoff and Johnson 1999: 20; Rohrer 2005; Ellestrom 2010a: 73–100). And what is spatial is characterized by properties like distance, relation, motion and proportion (Starr 2013: 40, 91; Ellestrom 2010a: 79); qualities that also signify rhythm. The diagrammatic icon connects the sensorimotor impulses of a poem to the thoughts and feelings of the reader and, in this way, also to their comprehension of the world. Poetic rhythm works within this field. A forward movement is inherited in the quick iambs, but a full stop enters when binarity proceeds to a closing spondee:

| l. 11 | A forest fire smouldered out. | o O o O o / O o O |
| | One by one cafés shut. | O o O / o OO |

These cafés are shut, indeed.

Synaesthesia denotes steady connections between the senses: sight, hearing and touch. The Swedish poet and Nobel Prize winner Tomas Tranströmer names the song of the blackbird a hieroglyph, which thereby transforms something that is heard to something seen. More than this, the hieroglyph is a perfect description of this special bird's song. Obviously, it is quite easy to transfer impulses between the senses, and the synaesthesia ability seems to be premodal.[5] Forms are established before they become heard or seen or felt.

## Biorhythms

Biorhythms constitute a special kind of diagrammatic icon. The body has silent methods for colouring life with feelings, attitudes and bodily memories from early childhood, from basic to all forms of signification. Rhythms in a piece of art will always be influenced by bodily knowledge, and biorhythms play a

---

[5] In Hopsch and Lilja 2017: 'An "i" is conceived as light, small and pointed, but an "a" is big and dark. Soft sounds are associated with dark, diffuse colours and big, round forms. What is misty, unclear, and soft belong together, like brightness and descant sounds. A long sequence of "a"s make the reader feel a certain weight. This phenomenon adds signification to a poem.' Here I refer to Jakobson and Waugh (1979: 183–7). Compare with Kühl's table in Chapter 5, p. 73 about the lapse precategorial – premodal – experienced.

prominent part in the signification process when reading a poem (Spitzer 2002: 227; Sonesson 2007: 115, 120; Starr 2013).

Poets often declare that they 'walk to get started'. Walking makes a rather regular rhythm, as is the case with other biorhythms like pulse and breathing. However, there seems to be a special quality in walking – like running, jumping – in respect to poetry. Maybe this is due to its many varieties and the choice of how to walk, such as quickly or slowly and so on (Pourcel 2010). Walking style can be most unconscious, quiet and regular, but it might also be a result of conscious choices. Walking is a biorhythm that allows irregularities as well as a full stop (if the poet wants to make a pause). All varieties signify something special – a jump may express joy or horror depending on the circumstances; this could occur unconsciously but also with full awareness. One runs for one's life in a regular, quick and jerky rhythm. Also, the verse line moves in some way, such as rising or falling, walking or balancing, regular or not.[6] Sequences of free verse, which are not so regular in rhythm, might be formed out of motor schemas like jumping or resting.

| Jumping | l. 10. | Bled seeds across its work-light. | oO / o O o O0 |
| Resting | l. 3:1. | Rain and hay [and woods on the air] | O o O / |

Other biorhythms seem to be aesthetically active as well. Interestingly enough, the time spans of different biorhythms coincide to a high degree, and these intervals return in ordinary versification categories. The approximate three-second interval of a common verse line and the three-second interval of the short-term memory coincide with the expiration interval – the time of a breath (Pöppel and Turner 1983). The pulse seems to have something to do with the serial rhythm of metered versification, but the tactus interval of half a second comes, approximately, even closer to the interval of the brain's echoic memory (Spitzer 2002: 116). Moreover, the half second of a normal step agrees with the time span of one tactus. So, this half second relates to many body rhythms such as heart beats, the steps of walking, as well as the echo memory – it is not so odd that the tactus pattern appears to be this strong (see also Ch. 8).

| | l. 13. | I thought of you continuously | oO oO oO o0 o |

I would say that these sensorimotor experiences, the biorhythms, dominate the signification process of verbal acoustics. Among them walking, jumping,

---

[6] Tsur (2012b: 26, 123) refers to Persinger (1987) when talking about the temporal lobe's role in the sensation of balance and movement.

dancing and so on should be the most important. A dancing body may express heaviness or ease, which are two very different shapes (Olsson 1993: 43). Such is the case with verse lines – to be expressed with the syllable stress ratio (SSR). Compare an easy line with a heavy one:

| | | | |
|---|---|---|---|
| l. 13. | I thought of you continuously | o O oo / o O ooo | SSR 4.5 |
| l. 8. | Each place granting its name's fulfilment. | OOO o / o O o O o | SSR 1.8 |

Thereby, I would say that our bodies are our best tools for reading poetry.

## A model for interpretation

We have seen that the semantics of rhythm deals with a countless number of tiny details. Every syllable takes place in this game, and each one works in a number of contexts. See, for example, the cited line 13. This may demonstrate alternation as well as easiness. Both readings are correct but from different perspectives – the light second and fourth stress may easily be suppressed but also accentuated if desired. This overwhelming amount of information has probably aggravated interpretations out of form impulses. However, this short exposition above gives us some hints about how to work when going from a specific rhythm to a specific emotion – from a pause to stability, and so on.

Here, I concentrate on phrase rhythms, but, as a matter of fact, rhythms make the same patterns even in larger scales, like stanzas and the whole poem; anyhow, pattern conception takes place within the time limit of the short-term memory, which is three seconds. The small phrase models the organization of the strong and weak material within the mind. Tiny subtleties decide the flow of significance when rhythms construct signification. A forward direction might be angrily tough or depressingly slow. A model for reading the rhythm consists of four steps as follows:

- The element of form constitutes movement – I identify the movements.
- The movement has a certain character – like speed or forwardness.
- This character in turn depicts a certain emotion – like joy or panic.
- The emotion then is specified according to the context.

The last point needs a comment. I have noted already that a figure with a certain set of qualities may be able to support different contexts. The joy and panic that are mentioned in the third point use rather similar biorhythms (cf. Tsur 2012b: 140–43). In both cases, the feeling moves fiercely, strong, up and down; a pattern with these qualities may support quite dissimilar contexts. A forceful movement may characterize joy as well as panic, and the context will decide which one it will be.

|  | | | | |
|---|---|---|---|---|
| | I thought of you continuously | o O oo / o O ooo | 9 | 2 |
| l. 14 | A thousand miles south where Italy | o O o OO / o O oo > | 9 | 4 |
| | Laid its loin to France on the darkened sphere. | o O o O / oo O o O | 10 | 5(4) |
| l. 16 | Your ordinariness was renewed there. | OOoOoo / oo OO | 10 | 5(4) |

Above, line 13 exemplifies both a sleeping tactus pattern and a lightness with two stresses only in a line of nine syllables. The SSR here will be as much as 4.5 (normal is just below 3). The initial figure oOoo (the second paeon) is repeated twice, with small variations in the second half line and in line 14:2 where it is followed by an enjambment. The interpretation schema shows how this works. Both the half lines of line 13 are mildly rising, but the repetition imposes a resting balance.

Line 14 is more uneven. There is a stop after the first half line, while the second one continues over in the next line 15. Reading an enjambment means to somewhat lengthen the last possible syllable before the break; here 'It-', and the usual pause of a half second in the very break disappears or shortens. In this way, the word 'Italy' will be emphasized. Here is a strong forward direction but the stop in the middle adds intensity and some kind of alarm.

If line 13 vaguely rises, this rising movement is fortified in line 14, and also reinforced with the help of the enjambment. One is somewhat thrown into the sensuous line 15 where it is possible to choose a stress on the first word or not. The enjambment calls for a stress here in order to fill up the line break pause, but one may also favour the rhythmical sameness of the two rising half lines of line 15, ooOoO. One can also feel a sleeping tactus that is independent of whatever reading is chosen.

If I take the rising interpretation, then the direction is fierce, but, simultaneously, a balance between the half lines extenuates the rush, and the augmented line length of ten syllables brings the same effect of expanded time.

An initial stress in line 15, however, fortifies that of line 16. Being a pronoun, 'Your' should normally not be stressed, but here it is acting as stress in contrast to the 'ordinariness' of the opening line 1, thus becoming the most important point of the whole poem. The line hangs in its two spondees; the initial one and the closing one, and between them all syllables are more or less weak. The spondees of line 16 repeat the one in line 14 and provide the poem's closure. The line stands still, resting in balance.

I have discussed this stanza line-by-line and investigated how its rhythm influences significance and lexical meaning. Repeated figures construct coherence and reinforce rhythmical tendencies.[7] Rising rhythm gives a forward direction, that here is abruptly stopped with the last line and its deviant construction. In the rhythmical signification of this stanza, some emphasis cooperates with a rather calm forwardness. The car moves forward and the rhythm illustrates this movement. The far distance to Italy is emphasized. As a whole, this poem is firmly directed at the saying of the last line, where rhythm also stays and creates a closure.

---

[7] Repeated figures in this stanza: 2nd paeon oOoo l. 13, 13, 14, sleeping tactus l. 13, 15, spondees l. 14, 16, 16 and anapaest plus iamb oo O o O l. 15, 15.

# 4

# Temporal and spatial rhythms: The intermedia perspective

## Forms are temporal and visual

In the Introduction (pp. 1–2) I described the ancient art form of *mousikē,* where dance, music and poetry form a whole. All these art forms consist of ordered courses of events. The very word 'rhythm' originates from the market place in Athens where a body moves in artistic order (Plato [1926] 1952; cf. Introduction pp. 1–2). Imagine the poet at the *agora* in this chapter – moving, playing and reciting; a body in time as well as space.

This is about rhythm in modern poetry. However, rhythm is important in all forms of art. Rhythm has aspects of time as well as space. Think of a Breughel picture where many small figures are busy with different tasks like shoeing a horse – works that take place in time, but the picture itself is a limited square.[1] The observer is met with time as well as space. Sound perception is primarily a matter of time, but visibility takes place in space. Movements involve both time and space. In the Breughel picture, time and space merely seem to complement each other.

The visuality of a poem can mean different things. Literature always has a base in visuality – one envisages images when reading (Starr 2013: 69). Metaphors are yet another kind of image in poetry. Multisensory imagery is the norm for a reader, thus aiming at something broader than only words.[2] Memory combines experiences and perceptions to a web of multisensory associations (Starr 2013: 51). Versification studies, however, is mainly interested in the visuality of the printed picture.

---

[1] I would like to thank Rudolf Rydstedt, Gothenburg University, for this example. I am also grateful for the suggestions of my late colleague Lena Hopsch at Chalmers Technological University, Gothenburg, who taught architectural students how to handle the rhythms of a facade.
[2] Visual images use brain areas that are normally used for planning our own motions. Motor imagery promotes human development, especially social cognition (see Starr 2013: 82).

As a whole, the relationship between visuality and temporality seems to be tight and complicated. I am moving in a room, and this movement influences space as well as time. Going for a walk uses both distance and time, but in this case the spatial movement appears to be more important than the time used. As already said, reading a poem may easily be compared with strolling along a path in the woods (Lakoff and Johnson 1999: 33). Neurologically, hearing and time have a weaker support than sight and place (Starr 2013: 72). This fact produces the peculiarity that one uses sight to understand time. One looks at a watch and the calendar. However, the bing-bong of church bells takes place in time, which is perceived with the help of our ears.

The poet Fredrik Nyberg writes in his dissertation that sight and hearing work simultaneously when writing a poem (Nyberg 2013: 481). The shapes of letters, words and pages stand close by that which was produced by the mouth and ear. Traditionally, audibility has been thought to be the dominant sense in poetry, but this can be debated. Together, the eyes and ears control the shaping of a poem, says Nyberg. There seems to be a reciprocal dependence between senses.[3] All precategorial sensorimotor-emotive processes are involved in the creation of poetry, as is true of all art (Kühl 2007: 50).

## Premodality

During the past century, the gestalt laws have been developed and alluded to in different ways. Classical principles of grouping, such as those mentioned in Chapter 2 (p. 28), have had additions like synchrony, common region and uniform connectedness – not to forget the role in contour completion (Kubovy and Valkenburg 2006). Jean Piaget studies how babies acknowledge perception schemas with the help of experience, and how these schemas coordinate and develop with time. They offer a possibility to preserve human experience (Piaget [1936] 1953: 47–143). Richard Cureton modernizes the principles of grouping by renaming them 'preference rules' (Cureton 1992: 191). Reuven Tsur discusses strong and weak gestalts as well as back-structuring (Tsur 2008).

The gestalt laws are the same for any form of art, even if they have historically been referred to as visual gestalts (Arnheim 2004; Starr 2013: 48). The same

---

[3] Listening to words produces visual and auditive representations in the reading mind. Short-term memory works visually as well as auditively (Murray 1995: 95–6).

perception process works in the meeting with music, poetry, visual art forms and the movements of the dancing body (Starr 2013: xv, 69). Aesthetic rhythms seem to use the same patterns for spatial and temporal art forms. One may conclude that perception schemas are *premodal* (cf. Ch. 5).

'Modality' can be understood as sign systems or technologies for representation. Lars Ellestrøm distinguishes between four kinds of modality: material, sensorial, spatiotemporal and semiotic (Ellestrøm 2010b: 15). My examples in this chapter, a poem and a picture, illustrate the spatiotemporal level, where time and space interact. According to Ellestrøm, the picture uses only three dimensions – width, height and depth – while poetry also needs a fourth one: time (Ellestrøm 2010b: 19). However, this classification is complicated by the fact that – from a perception perspective – the time dimension is interwoven with spatial qualities, and that visibility also needs time. Lakoff and Johnson explain this phenomenon with the conceptualization of motion. Motion takes place in space, and time will be conceptualized in terms of motion (Lakoff and Johnson 1999: 140). As already noticed, the perception process also adds time to the picture. However, a poem and a picture differ when it comes to the material and sensorial modalities.

Here, I will use approximately the same patterns for analysing visual and audible qualities – a Kandinsky picture and the printed picture of a Sylvia Plath poem, as well as the audible rhythm of the same poem. This is possible due to the premodal gestalt laws that behave basically the same in different art forms. Gestalts are just as important in audible courses of events as in visual ones and in tactile ones (Gallace and Spence 2011; Tsur 2012b: 198). From the perspective of intermedia studies, this is a crucial point. It is possible to use the same patterns for analysing rhythms in dance, sculpture, paintings, music and poetry. In all art forms, rhythms are moving and balancing.

Perception schemas structure the perceptions and give them coherence. Back-structuring decides the perceptual process, and the gestalt is only acknowledged when it is closed. The same patterns seem to be valid for all art forms. In the perception process, schemas occur before a differentiation takes place into visual, audible and tactile forms.[4] This means that spatial and temporal rhythm are basically the same (Starr 2013: 48, 88). Cognitive patterns and embodied experiences play crucial parts when one produces and perceives aesthetic rhythm.

---

[4] Mark Johnson and others refer to psychological experiments in order to prove what they call 'cross-modality' (Johnson 2007: 143). Compare with Rohrer (2005) for neural aspects.

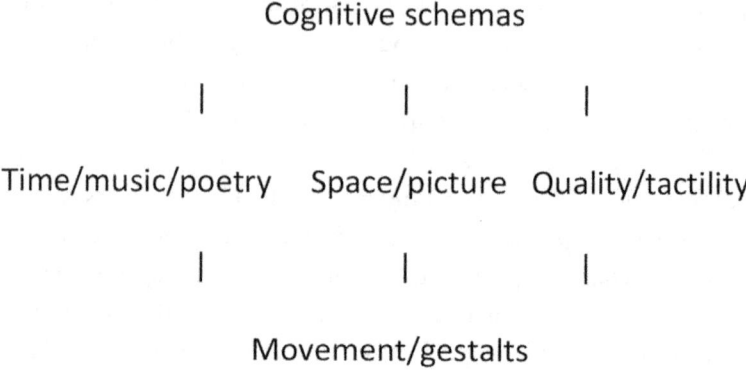

Figure 4.1 Cognitive schemas in time and space. Lena Hopsch and Eva Lilja. 2010. With permission by Michael Hopsch.

However, there are material and sensorial differences in the perception between temporal and spatial forms. As noted, some senses are spatially oriented, while others are temporal in character. Above I observed that spatial forms primarily meet as an entirety and then they need some time to develop the details. In contrast, temporal forms are first perceived in a lapse, but in a next step one is able to grip their wholeness, which spatializes the form. In poetry, the ear prefers the segment, and it will take us some time to catch the whole stanza or the space of the whole poem. The balance of a sculpture emanates out of (1) dynamic tensions, and (2) repeated sequences, which are both perceived in time. The balance of a poem emanates out of (1) repeated sequences, and (2) dynamic tensions in sound, semantics and typography.[5]

## Rhythm in pictures: Wassily Kandinsky

As already stated, the apprehension of spatial forms requires time to develop details. Lately, psychologists have measured people's eye movements when they are looking around, and one obvious result is that seeing takes time – there is also a time lapse to consider when looking at a picture (Peter Gärdenfors,

---

[5] Tsur discusses how the brain handles the reading process. Reading takes place in a narrow visual area of the brain, this in the left brain half that also uses a counterpart in the right brain half (Tsur 2017: 43–4).

personal communication, September 2010). At first, one fixes the gaze upon what is most important – mostly in the middle – after that advancing to the weaker parts of the image. Kandinsky's painting (Figure 4.2) will take some time to contemplate as the eye wanders from one side to another and back again. As for poems, they sometimes have expressive typography which influences the perception process.

The Kandinsky painting carries centres and directions. Wassily Kandinsky (1866–1944) is one of the most important artists of modernist abstract painting. The picture has two centres – the yellow door to the left might be its most important focus, but the dark forms to the right dominate as well. Having identified them, the eye will probably continue to investigate the three black circles – one close to the upper limit, one to the left of the door, and the small and very black one under the voluminous dark forms. After these main forms, one is prepared to consider the lighter lines and colours outside them.

What is rhythm in this painting? Well, there is a heavy movement in the dark volumes to the right of the picture. It starts from the middle-down and aims distinctly at the upper-right corner. The rectangular yellow door first seems to be a resting point, but a door is an opener, and something will happen if this

**Figure 4.2** Wassily Kandinsky, 'Gelb – Rot – Blau', 1925. © 2022. Photo Josse/Scala, Florence" in captions list in prelims.

door opens. The many thin lines close to the margins mostly point to the centre of the painting – they aim for balance. The same thing must be the case with the three dark circles that, to a certain degree, balance each other. But there is also a contrast between the heavy forms of the foreground and the light bluish colours of the background – somehow the dark burdens rest in a blue heaven. The rhythm here could be said to arise from a play between the forced direction forward and upward to the right and several forms that aim towards balance; just as between the sharp colours in the foreground and the light blue background, as well as a contrast between light – represented by the yellow door – and darkness.

In Kandinsky's books on art theory, he reflects on the possibilities of abstract forms to create significance (Kandinsky 1912; [1928] 1955). He starts with the square of the canvas, the basic surface – or as it is known in German, *Grund Fläche*. The left side means home while the right stands for distance, freedom and away – from the perspective of the public (Kandinsky [1928] 1955: 138). This is in accordance with the Western reading direction where one starts from the left side of a surface and is directed to the right side, in a forward direction. The same pattern is to be found in the typography of most early free verse – the left margin is stable but the right one wavers.

Kandinsky discusses the different tensions of various directions – left and right, up and down. Versification studies is also interested in directions, as in the rising forward direction and the falling backwards direction. A rising rhythm – iambs, anapaests – goes forward and supports clock time, but a falling rhythm – trochees, dactyls – is directed backwards to the left margin.

Kandinsky makes some observations concerning the signification of different directions – up and down where 'down' means the stable ground but 'up' is liberation, expansion and unknown possibilities (Kandinsky [1928] 1955: 131–3). This is to be compared with the cognitive metaphor of MORE IS UP, and its opposite of depressing downwards (Lakoff and Johnson 1980: 14). Cognitive semantics has ascribed the directions up and down to positive and negative meaning, respectively. The metaphor MORE IS UP means success but its opposite, LESS IS DOWN, is felt to be low-spirited. Here, cognitive semantics supports Kandinsky's ideas.

In addition, Kandinsky reasons about the qualities of different colours: red rushes but blue is calm (Kandinsky 1916). In Plath's poem below, red and blue are the dominant colours. Concerning the bright yellow door in the actual painting, Kandinsky thinks of yellow as a sign for earth, but blue means heaven. It seems correct to have this yellow form a little to the left (home), and the blue in the background may add a feeling of hovering in the air.

In the painting, there is a conflict between the resting forms in the middle left and the dark, heavy movement up to the right. 'Up' and 'right' should mean a determined statement of freedom and strength, but a threat emanates from the dark colours. Something black is breaking out regardless of the yellow door of lightness and safety. More than this, I find the three dark circles most expressive – they look like apocalyptic black suns (alluding to Kristeva's title of depression, *Black Sun*, [1987] 1989). In them, the harmonious circle is complicated by the dark colour. At the same time, they balance each other beautifully and evoke a dark, threatening power.

## A Plath poem

The notion of this chapter is that visual and audible rhythms could be analysed in much the same terms. Sylvia Plath's poem 'Poppies in October' has a funny title as poppies blossom in the beginning of the summer and should all be dead in October.

|  | Even the sun-clouds this morning cannot manage such skirts. |
| --- | --- |
| 2 | Nor the woman in the ambulance |
|  | Whose red heart blooms through her coat astoundingly — |
|  |  |
| 4 | A gift, a love gift |
|  | Utterly unasked for |
| 6 | By a sky |
|  |  |
|  | Palely and flamily |
| 8 | Igniting its carbon monoxides, by eyes |
|  | Dulled to a halt under bowlers. |
|  |  |
| 10 | O my God, what am I |
|  | That these late mouths should cry open |
| 12 | In a forest of frost, in a dawn of cornflowers. |

(Sylvia Plath, 'Poppies in October',
*Collected Poems*, 1981)

In my reading, this poem deals with a woman giving birth, and is now transported to a hospital. It is an early morning in October, and people are rushing to their jobs. The poppies of the title are never really mentioned, but some metaphors could be interpreted as poppies, the 'skirts' (l. 1), the 'gift' (l. 4) and the 'mouths'

(l. 11). Other red things are compared with poppies, such as the 'sun-clouds' (l. 1), the bleeding heart of 'the woman in the ambulance' (l. 3) and the flaming 'sky' of line 6–8. In the last stanza, the 'I' of the poem listens to the screaming of the poppies (l. 11).

The notation scheme of the phrase rhythm follows the straight norms of spoken language as much as possible, but of course my understanding of the poem will influence the scheme in details:[6]

|    |                              | **Stresses** |   |   | **Syllable stress ratio** |
|----|------------------------------|---|---|---|---------------------------|
|    | O oo OO OO o / oo O o OO     | 5 + 3 = 8 |   |   | 1.8  (1.6–2)              |
| 2  | O o O o / oo O oo            | 2 | 1 | 3 | 3                         |
|    | o OOO / oo O o O oo          | 3 | 2 | 5 | 2.2  (1.3–3.5)            |
| 4  | o O / o OO>                  | 1 | 2 | 3 | 1.9                       |
|    | O ooo OO>                    | 3 |   | 3 | 2                         |
| 6  | oo O>                        | 1 |   | 1 | 3                         |
|    | O oo O o                     | 2 |   | 2 | 2.5                       |
| 8  | o O oo O o O o 0 / o O >     | 4 | 1 | 5 | 2.2                       |
|    | O oo O oo O o                | 3 |   | 3 | 2.7                       |
| 10 | O o O / o OO                 | 2 | 2 | 4 | 1.8                       |
|    | o OOO / o OO o               | 3 | 2 | 5 | 1.6  (1.3–2)              |
| 12 | oo O oo O / oo O o O0 o      | 2 | 3 | 5 | 2.6  (3–2.3)              |

Here I have noted phrasal focus with the help of an extra bold ring. This is to highlight the phrasal directions. Prominences are counted per phrase and per line. The syllable stress ratio (see p. 14) tells if the phrase or line is heavy or light, that is, if it is dominated by stresses or by weak syllables. If the normal relationship is one or two weak syllables per stress, a stress ratio of 1.6 signifies an extremely heavy construction as the share of stresses is abnormal. A ratio of, for example, 3.5 is very light and depicts a line of mostly unstressed syllables.

The very first line of the poem is too long and too heavy to be stable. This line has an abnormal weight with eight prominences of 14 syllables. It is placed on a

---

[6] The cooperation between language stresses and narrative in a poem could be seen as a dialectic process. Figure 5.2 at p. 70 (see Chapter 5) describes how sound and significance build each other up throughout the text. See also 'How to read free verse' at p. 11 in the Introduction. When reading, some syllables must be stressed, others must not and then there is a third category where the circumstances decide what should be done. When I test different reading possibilities, I also discuss various alternatives to understand the text.

par with the extensive bottom line that is providing rest. However, this last line is lighter than line 1, it is a little shorter and carries a dancing series of anapaests – an easy-going rhythm.

Extra weight is given to lines 1, 4 and 10–11, as you can see in the right column. In these four lines the syllable stress ratio is less than 2, which is something that occurs rarely in naturally spoken language. Their weight points these lines out as the most significant passages of the poem. The poppies are introduced at the very end of line 1, which causes the rising movement of the line. A spondee situated immediately before the line break, which is the case in many lines here, will also create a rising motion. In the last stanza, lines 10–11 rather seem to stand still with their heavy burden of prominences.

Reversed directions of semantic and acoustic rhythms signify stanzas 2–3. The acoustic direction rushes forward with the help of strong enjambments, with one of them even bypassing the pause between stanzas (l. 6). The two stanzas consist of one long sentence that forms a falling unity on the semantic level. The 'love gift' of line 4 offers the hot centre of the passage; that which is most important emerges first in a falling figure. Line 4 also has extra acoustic weight (SSR 1.9) which strengthens the semantics. Semantic and acoustic rhythms are here in conflict, as the hot 'love gift' is presented in the beginning of the passage while rhythm is hurrying forward despite the fact that the most important thing has already been mentioned. The acoustic directions of the passage are mostly rising. Lines 4–5 are closed by spondees that give a heavy forward movement, just like the effects of the enjambments of lines 4–6 and 8 – and the last one is very strong. This means that semantic direction and line directions are in conflict in this part of the poem. The dactyls of line 9 will harmonize the passage.

To conclude, this poem distinguishes itself by extra weight. Spondees and enjambments add acoustic force, and the directions are mostly rising in a strong, forward movement. Force will cause a heavy rising rush – especially in the middle stanzas. These repeated movements balance each other, but within itself such a rising line is imbalanced. The rhythmical shape of this poem is indeed varied and active.

The visual rhythm is also interesting in this poem. The printed picture is characteristic for its epoch – a straight left margin and a wavering right one. The emptiness of the white paper is attacking the text – especially in stanza two. Here, I will try to unlock the visual rhythm with the help of three triangles.[7] The

---

[7] Lena Hopsch at Chalmers Technological University Gothenburg has designed the spatial analysis.

Even the sun-clouds this morning cannot manage such skirts.
Nor the woman in the ambulance
Whose red heart blooms through her coat astoundingly ----

A gift, a love gift
Utterly unasked for
By a sky

Palely and flamily
Igniting its carbon monoxides, by eyes
Dulled to a halt under bowlers.

O my God, what am I
That these late mouths should cry open
In a forest of frost, in a dawn of cornflowers.

**Figure 4.3** Sylvia Plath's poem inserted in triangles and squares by Lena Hopsch. 2010. With permission by Michael Hopsch.

printed picture of the poem is inscribed in a rectangle, or what Kandinsky would name a 'ground surface' (Kandinsky [1928] 1955: 129).

This square-shaped form may be parted in several triangular forms. The first one, standing on its base tip, follows the first and longest line of the poem, and has its back along the left margin. The second one takes the opposite view, resting on the bottom line that is also rather extensive. Both of them are strengthening the left margin which already forms a stable line. Together, they constitute two crossing diagonal directions that divide the rectangular surface, thereby balancing each other.

The third triangle has the tip of its toe down to the right, with one line under most of line 3 and another line delimiting the empty space to the right. This third one encloses the empty space of the centre. This third triangle is perhaps the most active. It also causes motion in the surface. The empty space in the middle of the surface highlights a visual imbalance.

The stanza lengths of this poem balance each other. There are three lines in every stanza, which is a regularity that plays with the forms of metered versification. Stanzas 1 and 4 are about balancing each other concerning line lengths. They are in balance due to their substantial size and heaviness, in contrast with the short rushing pair of stanzas 2–3.

I will use Kandinsky's observations for a better understanding of Plath's poem. The first line lacks stability, and is too long and heavy. As already said, this line has an abnormal weight, and it corresponds with the extensive bottom line. However, line 12 is lighter than line 1, it is a little shorter and uses cadenced anapaests. Kandinsky remarks that forms that hinder the upward freedom motion seem to be extremely blocking (Kandinsky [1928] 1955: 132). Moreover, he also discusses diagonal directions and separates between the harmonious down-left to the up-right diagonal one, as well as its opposite of the disharmonious down-right to the up-left one. This picture has them both, but the disharmonious direction dominates.

As previously mentioned, Kandinsky reasons about the qualities of different colours. The relationship between the red and the blue elements is a mystery in this poem. Red elements are the blood, poppies, mouths, etc., while the cornflowers of the last line are blue. According to Kandinsky, red rushes but blue is calm. The poppies colour everything in striking red, except for the last line where the blue cornflowers loosen its terror. Eleven shrieking lines are balancing on a small spot of blue quietness.

This poem delivers several messages. The heavy first line makes a slow start by introducing the bloodstained poppies. Then the rising motion grows faster to end up in the gallop of the third stanza (l. 7–8) which closes with a quieter row of falling dactyls. The heaviness of lines 10–11 makes this passage immovable. Here the reader is forced to linger. After this, the poem ends up with some anapaestic cornflowers (l. 12). Phrases repeat a couple of rhythmical patterns – spondees, dactyls – which produce tendencies to rhythmic stability.

I propose that the rhythmical analysis underlines some aspects of the narrative. A heavy forward dash could represent panic, and here it shows an ethos of terror. Perhaps like death rushing towards you. However, the last stanza breaks that hurry. The poppies are screaming, and time stands still.

Kandinsky characterizes red as the colour of rush but blue gives quietness. For eleven lines, the poppies paint the poem in red, but the twelfth line rests. The blue shade can be understood as a sign of the death of the woman, which would cooperate with the other surprise of the end line – namely the friendly anapaestic rhythm. This noisy and unruly piece ends in peace. Anapaests are mostly described as pacey and galloping, but these closing ones seem to bring some joy to the end with an easy-going forward movement. The childbirth may have ended happily, or just ended.

## Cooperation of modalities

I have now analysed some directions in a picture by Kandinsky, as well as the audible and visual parts of a Plath poem using categories like pattern and gestalt. Furthermore, I have talked about tempo, stability, directions and balance; all of which are things related to bodily movement. All these capacities seem to be premodal and work as well in visual as in audible forms. The same kind of patterns seem to be valid for the painting as well as for the poem.

Again, looking at and listening to the Plath poem, what is most striking here is the first line – it is too long and too heavy. I have pointed at some correspondence with the last, rather peaceful line. However, the printed picture of the poem is unstable because of the further length of line 1. Moreover, this line of fourteen syllables, which has a syllable stress ratio of 1.8, seems strikingly extreme. Kandinsky would say that this first line that is all too big stops any possibility of freedom and release as an upward motion is blocked.

The visual emptiness in the middle of the poem is also remarkable. To the left (stanzas 2 and 3), the audible rhythm gallops and to the right – the place of expansion and development – emptiness rules. Two diagonals cross the printed picture, where one stands for harmony and the other for its opposite, but the disharmonious one is so much stronger. What is seen and what is heard, cooperate in adding anguish to the woman's childbirth experience. Maybe death offers the only way to blue peace.

# 5

# Cognitive versification theory: Some aspects

## Cognitive schemas and gestalts

Rhythm is formed in a process, where reading adjusts the sounds of the poem. The acoustic registration differs a little from notations of what you really hear. The poet creates rhythms and figures, and the reader instinctively changes them a little.

Acoustic impulses are grouped according to gestalt laws (see Chapter 2) and *image schemas*. Mark Johnson, a philosopher in the Dewey tradition, explores how humans perceive the world out of sensorimotor experiences. His books investigate how the human body creates significance out of perceptions (Johnson 1987, 2007, 2018). Bodily experiences settle stable patterns of perception, thus creating unity and significance in the senses. The concept of image schema is crucial. An image schema stands for a bodily experience that is transferred into a stable pattern of perception (Johnson 1987: xix). In other words, the image schemas – here, cognitive schemas – are preconceptual structures that operate in the perceptual acts (Johnson 1987: 75; 2007: 35–36).[1] Impulses from the art work are ordered according to perception patterns in the receiving process. The means of versification trigger perceptual schemas that give basic form to gestalts that are not exactly the same as acoustic registrations.[2]

A poem, perceptual gestalts and sensorimotor cognitive schemas – this course forms a perception process. 'Rhythm' seems to be a matter of perceptions (cognitive schemas) that are triggered by impulses from the poem (gestalts) such as repetitions, tactus and other salient devices.

---

[1] As 'image schema' mainly refers to visual impressions, I have here chosen the label 'cognitive schema'. Manfred Spitzer supports Johnson when he understands aesthetic rhythm as an active process where the reader patterns the phrases and adds gestalt limits (Spitzer 2002: 216). Cf. Gibbs 2005: 90.

[2] Piaget uses the terminology somewhat differently. He used 'schema' for small entities and 'gestalt' for schemas that cluster, thus forming larger entities (Piaget [1936] 1953: 47–143). Generalized experiences develop intelligence. Gestalts bridge the body and mind (Piaget [1936] 1953: 137). Bridging tools are sensorimotor schemas (Piaget 1953: 122, 137). Piaget stresses the importance of perceptions and motor skills (Piaget 1953: 108, 119). The different senses depend on each other.

Johnson claims that our perceptions are formed according to sensorimotor experiences that produce patterns or cognitive schemas (Johnson 1987: xix). The shape and the significance of rhythm emanate from sensorimotor experiences – for example, experiences of the rhythms of the human body (Johnson 2018: 2; cf. Gallagher 2005: 14).

Instinctively, one pattern emerges before the others when deciding how to read a piece, and different readers mostly take the same one. The gestalt has no objective existence but is intersubjective (Tsur 2012b: 132). It is usually easy to agree on its shape even if it is formed in the individual perception. Choosing one gestalt before another probably means that this gestalt had the most components in common with the sound impulses.

Mark Johnson states that his schemas have gestalt characteristics, which is something that he defines as 'coherent, meaningful and unified wholes within our experience and cognition' (Johnson 1987: 41). Cognitive schemas and gestalts may thus be seen as two levels in the processing of perceptual impulses. Schemas direct the form of the gestalt and gestalts depend on schemas. In other words, schemas decide how to handle the perceptions and the result is shown in the gestalt.

## The nature of cognitive schemas

Johnson's notion of an image schema is a slight variation of Kant's concept of 'schema' (Johnson 1987: 147–57 – especially 153). However, there are also traces of gestalt psychology, especially that of Arnheim, but also ideas from Wittgenstein and Peirce (Ellström 2010b: 77, 79).

According to Johnson, cognitive or image schemas are mental mechanisms that form our experience of the world (Johnson 2007: 155–75; Trevarthen 2009).

> [I]n order for us to have meaningful, connected experiences that we can comprehend and reason about, there must be pattern and order to our actions, perceptions, and conceptions. *A schema is a recurrent pattern, shape, and regularity in, or of, these ongoing ordering activities* (Johnson 1987: 29).

Twenty years later, Johnson writes: 'Recurring, adaptive patterns of organism-environment interaction are the basis for our ability to survive and flourish. They are also the ground of meaning' (Johnson 2007: 136; see also Rohrer 2005: 165, 173).

Examples of basic schemas are CONTAINER, CENTRE, FORCE, DIRECTION, BALANCE, SOURCE-PATH-GOAL and so on (Johnson 1987). These patterns occur in versification. Sound impulses are ordered according to, for example, a forward-directed FORCE schema. Lines are patterned in BALANCE or, following the SOURCE-PATH-GOAL schema, running forward. This could be seen in the following discussion about Ferlinghetti's poem.

Johnson's explanations lean heavily on sensorimotor experiences, often biorhythms such as pulse, breathing, jumping and walking (Johnson 1987: 75; 2007: 35, 136). Many cognitive processes originate in repeated sensorimotor patterns (Johnson 1987: xix; 2007: 136). The experiences of the body create stable schemas that add unity and signification to new encounters between body and world. These schemas adapt the human being to the world as well as the other way around – the world to the human being, thereby organizing an interplay between mind and world. In common with these sensorimotor experiences are motion and movement, which is something that also constitutes the base of rhythmic experience (Starr 2013).

Lakoff and Johnson (1999: 103) distinguish between three levels of embodying our interaction with the world. There is a neurological level – we notice what our brains will allow us to notice (Johnson and Rohrer 2007: 32). The next level that follows is the very apprehension – what Lakoff and Johnson define as phenomenological (in the meaning of Merleau-Ponty). This is about perceptions, qualities, experiences and, by extension, culture and social circumstances. The third level consists of a postulated cognitive subconscious, including mental images, gestalt perception, semantic frames, motor skills, rhythms and cognitive schemas. These crucial functions show themselves with the help of their impact (Lakoff and Johnson 1999: 116).

One schema might be the base of many gestalts, and a verse line might be directed in many ways. For example, the last four lines of Ferlinghetti's poem '13' reveal both schema and gestalt in their rhythmic movement as follows:

|  |  | Schema | Gestalt | Figure |
|---|---|---|---|---|
| l. 20 | which is a laugh | O oo O | balance | choriamb |
| 21 | if you ask me | oo OO | direction | ionic |
|  |  |  |  |  |
| l. 22 | I too have drunk and seen | oO oO / oO > | direction | iambs |
| 23 | the spider | o O o | balance | amphibrach |

The stability of cognitive schemas has been called into question. Maybe the schemas work on a more ad hoc basis, which changes according to time and situation. This is a finding from the cognitive psychologist Raymond Gibbs, out of a series of psychological experiments. He discusses cultural categories, where the structures seem to be more dynamic (Gibbs 2005: 144). However,

## 13

        sweet and various the woodlark
              who sings at the unbought gate
and yet how many
            wild beasts
                  how many mad
   in the civil thickets
              Hölderlin
                      in his stone tower
or in that kind carpenter's house
                at Tübingen
      or then Rimbaud
            his 'nightmare and logic'
    a sophism of madness
    But we have our own more recent
                    who also fatally assumed
that some direct connection
              does exist between
    language and reality
              word and world
      which is a laugh
           if you ask me
    I too have drunk and seen
            the spider

**Figure 5.1** Facsimile of Lawrence Ferlinghetti, *A Coney Island of the Mind*, 1958. New Directions.

for the sake of versification I have reached another result – form patterns are definitely very stable if one considers the historical development. Once a verse pattern is created, it lives on in the depth of our cultural minds with an astonishing strength. In northern Europe, the perseverance of the four-beat line is a significant example. The power of seriality is another. Maybe form schemas are stable but cultural schemas are more volatile.

    The growing literature concerning cognitive schemas concentrates on issues such as concepts, classification, cause and other subjects related to signification.

However, the significance of form in this process seems to have been overlooked – something that Johnson has repaired in his latest book of 2018. A shift in emphasis in previous models could be as follows:

Johnson (1987) and others:    Schema – form – **signification**
Poetics/aesthetics:           Schema – **form** – signification

## A Ferlinghetti poem

The concluding poem '13' in Lawrence Ferlinghetti's collection, *A Coney Island of the Mind* (1958) discusses language theory in a most pleasant way. There are no stanzas to be seen, but four-line groups may be distinguished with the help of extra blanks, parting the text:

Line group 1–6:
Claims the wood lark to be the first among singers, which puts it in contrast to the 'wild beasts.'

Line group 7–13:
Mentions two of the beasts, Hölderlin and Rimbaud, perhaps the most elevated of all poets. Here they are declared beasts because they are said to be mad.

After line 13 comes the volta or the break of the poem, which now leaves nature as well as history and prepares for a conclusion.

Line group 14–19:
Describes the most common theory of language, the idea of a simple relationship between language and the visible world – the mirror theory or, maybe, naïve realism.

Line group 20–23:
Brings the problem to a conclusion by rudely rejecting this relationship, and pinpointing that you may see whatever – if you are intoxicated (or mad?) enough.

The notation schema below shows the play between rhythmic principle and cognitive schema. I have designated some rhythmic qualities per line. The first column notates stresses and weaks – this notation shows the speech rhythm. The second one goes back to the actual rhythmic principle – if the line uses tactus or sequence. In this table, I have dropped the dynamic qualities, but I will come back to them later. The third column shows the cognitive schema of the line – if it is directed or resting. DIRECTION as well as BALANCE are subschemas to FORCE, and I will comment on that below. The fourth column names the figures.

| | | | | |
|---|---|---|---|---|
| 1 | O o O ooo O0 | serial rhythm | direction | trochees |
| 2 | o O oo O0O | sequential | direction | molossus |
| 3 | o OOO o > | sequential | balance | molossus |
| 4 | OO | sequential | balance | spondee |
| 5 | O oo O | sequential | balance | choriamb |
| 6 | oo Oo Oo | serial | direction | trochees |
| — | | | | |
| 7 | O oo | sequential | direction | dactylus |
| 8 | oo OOo | sequential | balance | bacchius |
| 9 | O o OOO oo O | sequential | balance | molossus |
| 10 | o O oo | sequential | balance | second paeon |
| 11 | oO oO | serial | direction | iambs |
| 12 | o OO o O o | serial | balance | bachius |
| 13 | o O ooo O o | serial | balance | tribrach |
| — | | | | |
| 14 | oo O o OOO o | sequential | balance | anapaest, molossus |
| 15 | o O o O ooo O | serial | direction | iambs |
| 16 | o O o O o O o > | serial | direction | iambs |
| 17 | O o O o O > | serial | balance | trochees |
| 18 | O ooo O oo | serial | direction | trochees |
| 19 | O o O | sequential | balance | cretic |
| — | | | | |
| 20 | O oo O | sequential | balance | choriamb |
| 21 | oo OO | sequential | direction | ionic |
| 22 | oO oO oO > | serial | direction | iambs |
| 23 | o O o | serial | balance | amphibrach |

Chapters 10 and 11 will further explore the schemas of DIRECTION and BALANCE in free-verse poems. What is important just now is the internal relationships between various levels of rhythm production.

The style of the poem changes between the rather high-brow language of cultural tradition in the beginning, to ordinary speech in the second half. Also, the tempo changes between different parts of the poem. The second line group – that which handles Hölderlin and Rimbaud – starts in a slow tempo with sequential rhythm. The comments on Hölderlin include one slow spondee in line 8, and the next line, 9, carries a heavy molossus. When talking about Rimbaud, the rhythm – quicker and quicker – changes to the serial principle, reaching a full stop after line 13. The very last line group pictures the same curve. After the slow expressive ionic oo OO of line 21, follows the regular iambic tetrameter of the last two lines, which anchor the poem in its rash final conclusion.

The sequential free-verse rhythm dominates the first half of the poem, and serial rhythm becomes more and more dominant in the second half. Obviously, there is no simple relationship between the actual principle of rhythm and the cognitive schema of the line.

## FORCE schema and visual rhythm

Of course, dynamic rhythm is also at work in this poem. Regarding the semantic rhythm, there are a couple of prolongations in every part. For example, in the first line group 'the woodlark' makes a prolongation goal in lines 1–2, and 'wild beasts' in lines 3–6. However, dynamic rhythm works as well in the print picture of the poem.

This poem is spread over the paper more loosely than one would have been used to in 1958. Both margins are loosely waving in a way that differs very much from metered stanzas but also from early free versification with its typical picture – a straight left margin and a slightly wavering right margin. The blanks between the lines differ in extensiveness. Lines 3–11 make a loftier impression than the rest of the text, and the line group 12–19 is tighter and more concentrated. This latter part elaborates language theory in an informal spoken language, and here the printed picture goes tighter than before.

The picture differs also as regards broadness. It is rather slim in the beginning, but, especially, the tight part of the third line group gets obviously thicker. When it comes to iconicity, this poem might be compared with a fat-bellied fellow standing – not too steadily – on his right foot. The printed picture is unstable. It has two swings to the right and one to the left, as seen in the diagram. One dynamic FORCE hits the picture up to the right, another in the middle of the left, and a third one down to the right.[3]

---

[3] The diagram is made by Lena Hopsch, Chalmers Technological University, Gothenburg.

The field of image schemas has grown since Mark Johnson published his book in 1987. Some scholars have classified about twenty-five strong schemas that also have subordinated patterns (Hampe 2005: 2; Lakoff and Johnson 1999: 16–44). Our investigations have shown that the schema of FORCE is especially important in aesthetic analysis.[4] FORCE is connected to gravitation and its bodily reactions. Subordinated patterns to FORCE are, among others, DIRECTION and BALANCE, and these two are central for rhythm in all kinds of art.

Characteristics of the cognitive schema of FORCE are degrees of intensity as well as directionality, like a path with origin, goal and closure (Johnson

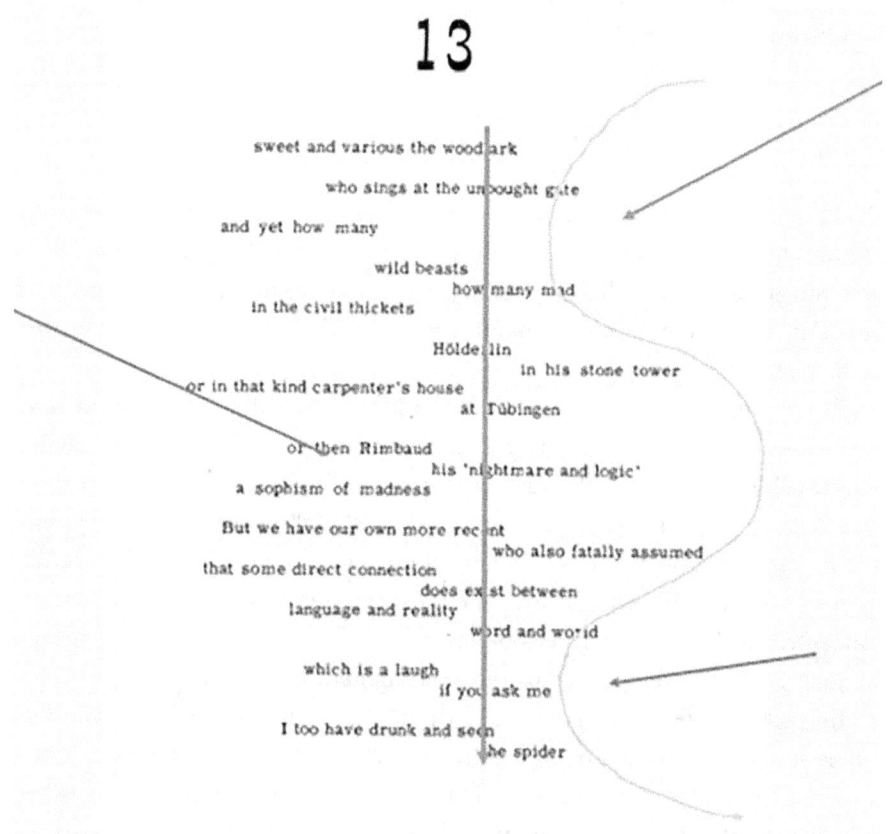

**Figure 5.2** Facsimile of a Ferlinghetti poem with directions inserted by Lena Hopsch. 1958, 2010. With permission by Michael Hopsch and New Directions.

---

[4] Lena Hopsch, Chalmers Technological University, Gothenburg and myself, during 2013–2018, analysed poems and visual artworks/sculptures from many perspectives.

1987: 43–4). The FORCE schema is basic and has many specifications – FORCE structures operate constantly in the experience. For example, they are common knowledge when taking a walk – a process of regularly leaving and returning to the ground. The FORCE schema can be specified in several ways and the force may be blocked. Johnson focuses on the strong and simple specifications of 'Compulsion' and 'Blockage', but there are also FORCE structures with two directions in play. 'Counterforce' could have reference to a car crash as well as to the balance of a tightrope walker. The weaker 'Diversion' could be illustrated by rowing in a headwind (Johnson 1987: 45–7).

The FORCE schema may be related to the traditional versification terminology of rising and falling rhythm. The forward direction of rising iambs and anapaests uses the compulsion schema to different degrees, but the falling, slow trochees have two forces in play – forwardness along with the reading direction and backwardness in leaving a strong position (Tsur 2017: 215). This happens according to the diversion schema.

The 'Blockage' schema is accompanied by the 'Removal of blockage' (Johnson 1987: 46–7). When these categories are transferred to the field of versification, it is possible to recognize the line break and its upheaval, the enjambment – a blockage and its removal. As already said, a line break defines versified form in relation to prose. This repeated pause, about a half second long, basically changes the conditions of reading and rhythm. The peculiar extensions and intonations of the enjambment – a phrase jumping over the line break – include compulsion, which is a strong directionality.

However, the very scene of FORCE in versification is the gestalt. As said before, the rhythm in a poem consists of gestalts:

> I too have drunk / and seen // the spider    (l. 22–23)
> oOoO            oO        oOo
> prolongation goal: 'the spider'

Gestalts are, by definition, closed and keep together with the help of perceptual forces emanating out of the part's relation to the borders and the whole (Tsur 2012a: 83, 86). 'Force' is a crucial theme in Gestalt psychology as well as in cognition studies. Smaller gestalts make parts of the bigger one. The citation here constitutes one gestalt (the line pair), as well as two gestalts (the two lines) and three gestalts (the three phrases). Forces work on all three levels. The first two phrases, that is the line, are dominated by the forward directed iambs. The prolongation goal comes at the very end of the line pair, shaping a strong forward direction through it.

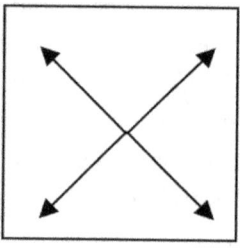 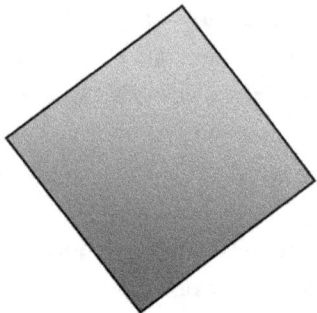

**Figure 5.3** Balance and tension in squares. By Lena Hopsch. 2010. With permission by Michael Hopsch.

A square contains directions out of its centre, which creates various tensions and movements, and so is, of course, the case with all kinds of forms – even the fat-bellied man of the actual poem.

As already said, a form has tensions and motions within its gestalt (e.g. Tsur 2011). Primarily, the parts of a gestalt relate to each other and not to something outside. A resting square is felt to be in equilibrium, motionless, when standing on one of its sides with its internal forces in balance. However, if standing on one of its angles, it would be felt to be moving. Oblique orientation is probably the most elementary and effective means of obtaining directed tension.[5] Ferlinghetti's unsteady print picture underlines qualities like flight (the woodlark rises from the ground up in the sky) or genial madness (Hölderlin and Rimbaud are really not squares) and a sarcastic, evasive grin in the end.

## Precategorial information and premodal patterning

Perception schemas are premodal, but what about the precategorial information of a poem – significations that emanate from the listening process in a moment before the emergence of the gestalts. Tsur calls it a background murmur beneath form (Tsur 2012b: 20–1). Here Tsur refers to Margaret Freeman's concept of 'minding'. Freeman speaks about a flux of perceptions before the objectification into concepts, and before awareness (Freeman 2009: 169–96 – especially 176).

---

[5] Lena Hopsch, Gothenburg Technological University, personal communication, 2005, 2017. Hopsch also drew the figure.

Tsur's book *Playing by Ear and the Tip of the Tongue* (2012b) analyses the precategorial perceptions. The book aims to explain the relationship between precategorial information and its semantic and phonetic circumstances. Like Freeman, he postulates a background mumble that is not categorized, but full of undetermined significance that originates from the context – and this context might be semantic as well as acoustic. A precategorial production of significance precedes the gestalt, he says. Sound may be coded as speech according to the left half of the brain, and as a non-speech mode according to the right half. The speech mode is strictly coded and fast, when sound changes a little according to codes. One will slightly hear something else other than what one really hears. However, with the help of a non-speech mode, one can really hear the very sound – the acoustics. Poetry allows us to take part in both speech mode and acoustics – a truly fantastic art form (Tsur 2012b: 194).

Ole Kühl's table below demonstrates the interrelation between the precategorial listening and the premodal patterning (Kühl 2003: 95; 2007: 90). The column shows how sounds, like phonemes and the tones of music, go into the perception process, which transduces into patterns of rhythm and – later – meaning. This process has three steps: the first is precategorial, the second is premodal and patterned, and the third has form as well as significance with the help of the long-term memory's experience.

The first square of the first line in Figure 5.4 stands for a rapid impulse that is slotted away to the NOW of the middle column, and – after that – to the final coding with the help of experience. The second line is about the time span that is needed, and the third line is about the development of signification. Tsur, as well

| **Precategorial perception** | **Premodal patterning** | **Form and meaning** |
| --- | --- | --- |
| Perception | NOW | Experience |
| 0.5–3 seconds | About 3 seconds<br>Short-term memory | More than 3 seconds<br>Long-term memory |
| Possible signification | Signification | Experience determines the signification |
| Phonemes, tones etc. | Schema, gestalt, word, Phrase | Lines and clauses |

**Figure 5.4** Interrelation between precategorial listening and form/meaning. 2003. Danish original by Ole Kühl, expanded and translated.

as Freeman, would say that some significance from the precategorial perception will be saved in this process. The meaning of this rapid impulse will quickly develop into the premodal patterning that will become fixed in the long-term memory. The last line states the language level; first a lonely phoneme, after that words and phrases, and lastly lines and clauses.

Chapter 4 has already discussed premodality – the second column – in relation to temporal and visual art forms. Another aspect is the premodal level of reception before the form is fixed. Poetic rhythm is processed in the short-term memory where it is limited and recoded, grouped and articulated (Tsur 2012a: 76). Of course, the choice of schema happens instinctively, influenced by the reminiscence of some movement that has arisen due to the actual perceptions, as well as the environment and memory (Gibbs 2005: 74).

The third column aims at long-term memory with its accumulated experience. Of course, rhythms are part of these experiences; for example, biorhythms. Long-term memory functions on various levels (Murray 1995: 112–14; Spitzer 2002):

- Silent knowledge like feelings, movements, muscle memory
- Episodic memory, narratives, coherence
- Semantic memory, significance and lexical meaning.

Impulses will be recoded in the long-term memory in chunks or gestalts in order to plug into the collected experience.[6] The first group, silent knowledge, embraces the biorhythms. The second level, the episodic memory, ensures that information that does not match the actual narrative will disappear. The third case, the semantic memory, seems to dominate the signification process – it is much easier to recollect significance and semantic meaning rather than pure sound (Murray 1995: 98).

---

[6] Here David Murray (1995: 96) goes back to George Miller's idea from 1956 of ideally sized chunks; the so-called 'magic seven' (Miller 1970).

# 6

# Levels and times

## Levels

The line of about three seconds is the most important gestalt of a poem, but of course there are shorter as well as longer gestalts to be aware of. The different levels use various amounts of time, and I will now reflect a little on the concept of time in poems. In Chapter 2 (p. 27) I stated that seasons as well as solar systems are perceived within the short-term memory frame of about three seconds, which is why they depend on the same kind of patterning as poetry. However, there is a play between the different levels of rhythm and thereby also between the levels of time in a poem.[1]

A poem has at least four rhythmical levels: the whole poem, the stanza, the line and the phrase.

- The printed picture    visual rhythm
- Stanza                 visual and audible rhythm
- Line                   audible and visual rhythm
- Phrase                 audible rhythm

Looking at the poem as a whole, the printed picture will dominate the impression, and the rhythm will be primarily visual – provided that you read it silently, which is mostly the case with modern poems. As for the stanza, rhythm is also visual, but you might hear its structure. The ordinary line (of mostly two phrases) is small enough to form an audible gestalt, but you can also see it. The rhythm of a phrase, however, cannot be grasped by the eyes – the rhythm is only

---

[1] Compare with Cureton's three rhythmic components that also use various amounts of time (Cureton 1992: 126–53). About rhythmic hierarchies, see Cureton 1992: 122.

temporal. The small audible phrase of the first line in the Leonard Cohen poem below makes an amphibrach:

> l. 1   You need her                                  o O o

Of course, such a figure could be projected over larger parts of a poem with a strong middle part and a weaker beginning and ending. The poem below could be described as a figure of the fourth paeon, ooo O, with three weaker parts before its centre of gravity. A piece of art consists of gestalts of various sizes with layers upon layers that influence and consociate with each other. The bigger one embraces many smaller figures as is to be seen in the poem below.

There are certainly no strict rules here, for example slam poetry is only audible in all its varieties. Concerning the stanza, its size and specificities decide how it will be treated, and so on. But at least four levels of a poem – see above – are patterned in bigger and smaller gestalts. One can describe its rhythm in detail at a minimum of four levels (Cureton 1992: 151). What is strong at one level might be weak at another one. The final rhythmic interpretation will weigh it all together; something that every reader does automatically. This could be seen in line 7 in the poem below:

>       And she said, I for one       oOO / OoO >
> l. 7  am happy with the world    o O ooo O            o O o O o O

In this line pair there are traces of an underlying serial rhythm that is inherited from the previous line pair of 4–5. Because of this vague tactus, the reader can alternate from the comma in line 6 to the end of the line pair. In that case 'with' in line 7 would be given extra stress. However, the strong bacchius oOO in the very beginning of line 6 demands speech rhythm, and when weighed together – I will suggest – line 7 should be read with some extra strain on 'with' – but without an outspoken tactus. When read in a straightforward manner, 'with' should be unstressed but, with regard to the rhythmic context, a slight tactus might appear in this line.

So, every detail enters into several rhythmic gestalts of various sizes. Some patterns are repeated, others contrasted. In the hierarchy of the four levels, patterns of phrase relate to patterns of the stanza and of the whole poem. The bigger gestalt influences and changes the pattern of the smaller one.

## A Cohen poem

We have already touched on the Cohen poem, No 55 from his *The Energy of Slaves* (1972).[2] It will act as our starting point for discussing levels and periodic time.

|    | You need her | o O o | |
|----|---|---|---|
| 2  | so you can get | ooo O > | |
|    | your boots off the bedspread | o O oo O0 | |
|    |   |   |   |
| 4  | We who have always ruled the world | O oo O o / O o O | iambs |
|    | don't like the way you dance | o O o O o O | iambs |
|    |   |   |   |
| 6  | And she said, I for one | o OO / O o O > | |
|    | am happy with the world | o O ooo O | |
|    |   |   |   |
| 8  | She seized the lapel of a cut-throat | o O o O o / oo O0 | |
|    | and said it again | o O oo O | |
| 10 | with all her small voice trembling, | o O o OOO o | |
|    | I for one am happy with the world | O o O / o O ooo O | trochees |
|    |   |   |   |
| 12 | I don't know if I want to kill her or not | oo O oo O / o O oo O | anapaests |
|    |   | o OO o OO / o OO o O | bacchii |

(Leonard Cohen, No 55, *The Energy of Slaves*, 1972)

I have to start with the messy pronouns. I will suggest that the speaker is the 'you' of the first two line groups and the 'I' in line 12. The other person here, a woman, could be the 'she/her' of lines 1, 6, 8, 10, 12 as well as the 'I' of lines 6 and 11. Who, then, is the 'we' of line 4? Perhaps exactly what the line says, 'We who have always ruled the world', a superior everyman, who is obviously in some way related to the woman of the story. 'She' and 'we' together are forming an enemy of the protagonist hooligan; all of the hostile society.

The story of this poem concerns a man, who calls himself 'a cut-throat' and lives with a woman, who represents societal order. She states that she is loyal to 'the world' – perhaps the middle-class order. The man gets very irritated and ponders on killing her. This last saying could be ironic or not. There is a conflict

---

[2] I would like to thank Ulf Cronquist, PhD, Gothenburg University, for providing several ideas about the analyses of this poem.

of class as well as a conflict of gender. The poem centres on the psychology of the male character.

There is a strong tendency towards iambic reading in many lines (l. 1, 2, 4, 5, 7, 8 and 9). Line 11 alternates as well, but is falling. Then there are passages that are opposing of any tactus, like the bacchii of lines 6 and 12 and the molossus of line 10. But here it would also be possible to read with tactus with the price of some distortion.

Many lines in this poem coincide with the phrase, but there is also the more normal case of two phrases in the line (l. 4, 6, 8, 11 and 12). As a whole, stanzas and prolongations cooperate:

l. 1–3: A forward direction. Prolongation goal: 'need her'.
l. 4–5: A forward direction in iambic tactus. The commencing choriamb is common in iambic verse and does not disturb its forwardness. Prolongation goal: 'don't like'.
l. 6–7: A forward direction. The latter line has a vague iambic tact. Prolongation goal: 'happy'.
l. 8–11: Here comes the emphatic core of the poem and the rhythm is nuanced. The molossus of line 10 'her small voice trembling' oOOOo parts the poem into a before and an after – as a kind of prolongation goal for the poem as a whole as well as for the stanza.
l. 12: A forward direction. There are two possible readings regarding semantics as well as rhythm. The line is ambiguous and could be understood in two ways, but both possible readings are directed forward, with anapaests ooO or rising bacchii oOO. This line closes the poem effectively. Prolongation goal: 'kill her'.

The narrative cooperates with the rhythm of the poem – there are narrative structures at both these levels. According to Aristotle's poetics, every story has (at least) a beginning, a climax and a closure, and any Hollywood film follows that rule. The same kind of movement is to be found in courses of rhythm that build up to a culmination and thereafter ebb away. In this way, a piece of music, for example, tells a story about going somewhere, finding something and then relaxing (Kühl 2003: 59). The same emotional pattern – with variations of course – exists in poetry and any other kind of rhythmic contexture. Here, I would suggest that the molossus of line 10 makes the culmination of this poem and plays an important part in the structure of the poem as a whole. The molossus stands still – a balance point:

l. 10   with all her small voice trembling,                    o O o OOO o

The line pictures the girl as a weak person, however, she is brave enough to challenge the man. From this line, the reader gets a hint of what keeps this odd couple together. From the perspective of the protagonist hooligan, the phrase also expresses contempt and scorn for the girl – or perhaps for the whole middle-class establishment.

According to direction, rhythm and narrative cooperate. Most of the rhythm here goes forward on the level of the phrase and the line. As already said, an iambic tactus is the dominating rhythmic device of this poem – within the frame of a free verse, of course. Also, the story about the irritated hooligan quickly runs forth to the bad solution(s) of the last line. The course of events skips insignificant details to concentrate on the important moments. There is a rush both in form and story.

However, the forward movement holds back with the repetition of lines 6–7 in line 11:

l. 11   I for one am happy with the world                O o O / o O ooo O

This sentence appears twice with varied line breaks. The syllable stress ratio of line 6 counts as low as 1.5, which is something that marks it out as an important saying. The repetition of line 11 is the only falling passage of this poem. Falling direction goes slower and takes more time than the rising iambs (Tsur 2017). So, in various ways, the girl's replica is marked as crucial.

A repetition breaks a straightforward movement by turning back to the first occurrence – in a poem the end rhyme is the simplest example of this common poetic structure (Jakobson 1960: 358). Repetition facilitates reading, when creating and closing a gestalt, which here consists of lines 6–11. That which is in between the two occasions will be kept together in the reader's mind.

Irony characterizes Cohen's songs and poems, and this is the case in this poem. It follows slightly through the story. The last line also allows us to comprehend all of the poem, if devices of rhythm support irony.

'Irony' is defined as (at least) two layers of meaning that are fighting each other. You say something but at the same time you signal that the very opposite should be understood. This could be done in many ways, using so-called irony markers; that is, something in the saying sounds inadequate and the reader has to look for a saying other than the obvious one (Booth 1974: 49–76). Rhythm may work as an irony marker.

There are many irony markers in this poem before the crucial last line. The first comes in line 3, where the concern about the bedspread seems too simple to form the basis of a serious relationship; this is an understatement that signals an irony marker. The next stanza lines 4–5 uses an iambic tactus. However, its saying sounds a little peculiar. I have already pointed out that one cannot be sure who the speaker is. However, I suggested that the 'we' of line 4 alludes to the snotty middle class. In this free-verse poem, the suddenly very cadenced iambs of lines 4–5 surprise the reader. Furthermore, they do not cooperate very well with the content of the saying. All in all, the iambs here are too strongly stressed for the saying and, in this way, they form an irony marker. The strong tactus estranges the snotty middle class, and there are two layers of meaning – a condemnation of the hooligan at the surface level and a condemnation of the prissy speaking 'we' in the subtext.

Line 8 begins the more nuanced part of the poem, leaving the iambs for a rising ionic oo OO at its very end '… of a cut-throat' (this figure repeats the ionic in the end of line 3, 'off the bedspread' oo OO, in a kind of rhyming effect). This salient figure accentuates the protagonist as a murderer – or is this perhaps irony? Maybe the subtext notifies the bedspread as his only victim.

Line 12 might be read in two different ways – either straight or ironically, and here the rhythm chosen decides the very sense of the whole poem. It could be interpreted with galloping anapaests or with emphatic bacchii – and of course maybe something in between.

l. 12   I don't know if I want to kill her or not    oo O oo O / o O oo O    anapaests
                                                     o OO o OO / o OO o O    bacchii

The bacchii reading takes the situation seriously – the man really ponders cutting the girl's throat – when the anapaest reading makes it all a joke. Like in lines 4–5 a chanting tactus conquers the literal saying, which evokes a subtext that opposes the factual meaning of the sentence. The bacchius kind of gestalt, including two stresses close together, underlines what is said, brings down the syllable stress ratio and slows down the tempo, while anapaests work the opposite way. Galloping anapaests suppress literal meaning as well as nuanced understanding, because they arouse the hypnotic qualities of serial rhythm. The drumming and dancing dervish in the first place listens to his body. In Germanic languages, the weak parts of an anapaest occupy very little time and together they are shorter than the strong syllable of the figure, something that creates distortion (Tsur 2017).

The trembling voice of the girl (l. 10) uses no irony – its emphatic molossus also gives to the rest of the poem a bleeding heart. This molossus makes its protagonist a living and feeling human, not a murderer, and this means that line 12 should be read with ironic anapaests. The forward direction dominates the rhythm of the poem as a whole, but, more than that, the two stanzas (l. 6–11) form a circle with the help of repetition.

All four levels of rhythm – phrase, line, stanza and the whole poem – are of course important for the impression of a poem, but the line and its approximate size of three seconds is the main category (see Chapter 2, p. 27). These three seconds constitute the size of the short-term memory, the amount of time possible to keep in the mind simultaneously (Pöppel 2004).

Any pattern forms itself within this limit. When the reading of a poem comes to its end, it will be back-structured (Tsur 2012a: 302). Suddenly one has perceived its form and in the same moment patterned it (Smith 1968: 2). Well, one might need a couple of reviews before the poem appears in all its glory. The gestalts are formed within this three-second interval to be projected over stanzas and the whole poem. Here I talk about form, but of course the same process takes place regarding meaning.

## Time

The projecting of patterns from the short-term memory of three seconds over larger levels in the poem complicates the concept of time (Muldoon 2006; Hoy 2009). Everyone is always captured in the now, knowing nothing about the past and even less about the future. The phenomenologist Maurice Merleau-Ponty writes beautifully about time and now. Time behaves like the water jet of a fountain, he says, all the time new water appears but the jet is the same. One knows nothing about the water source or where the water goes (Muldoon 2006: 119–78). However, I doubt this saying. Obviously, everyone knows a lot about the past as well as being aware of the future.

Past and future exist as memories and in the imagination (Lakoff and Johnson 1999: 137–69). I can see them as pictures, without a timeline, but in scenes. Evidently, it is impossible to move back in time; however, moving backwards functions very well in space. As said before, rhythm is basically modelled on body movement, and one moves in time and in space just as well – perhaps even easier in space. The experience of regression in time – something that happens when reading poetry – makes the reader apprehend time as if it were space (Lakoff and Johnson 1999: 139–40).

In our mental worlds, all of life is embraced by small and big gestalts. If moments consist of well-formed formal and cultural gestalts, these could provide access to the past as well as to the future. When standing in the middle of a pattern, any second contains things from the past, like a substantial bunch of material that also give some knowledge about the future. One patterns the coming days according to the material one already has. I plan for an excursion on the weekend and then I perform it. Plans for the week start on Monday, to be a closed gestalt on Sunday evening. The rhythm of a poem makes a gestalt that will be closed. Half-way through my reading, I understand, approximately, what the closure will look like (Smith 1968: 2). Regarding the immediate gestalt, I can understand the future using materials from the past – I stand in the middle of a gestalt even if it is only for three seconds.

The gestalt seems to function as a way to retain more information than really should be possible. A digit series will be almost impossible to remember – however, if they are well grouped, or patterned, it is easy (Spitzer 2002: 126). Facts behave in the same way, which is something that is demonstrated in the narratives of oral societies, where stories are used to transfer important knowledge between generations (Ong [1982] 2002). Such narratives increase the amount of time that is possible to grasp. When grouping digits, facts or other things, one builds contextures that help mental capacity. But the very grouping happens within the frame of three seconds.

## Time of different kinds

What is called 'time' really consists of many different phenomena. In the first place, there is clock time which measures time in an unvaried and scientific manner. In this timescape, entropy guarantees a beginning and an end of the world. The direction must invariably point forward. However, looking around in nature, time seems to be more periodic – spring returns each year, new children are born and old people die. Society, for its part, manipulates time, organizes it and intensifies it by creating weeks of seven days, vacation periods, Christmas, and so on – here time is more of a social construction.[3] Psychological time

---

[3] Lately, social sciences has studied societal time and named it 'temporalities'. This kind of time seems to be a mixture of the three others mentioned here.

appears to be rather different from clock time (Fraisse 1963). In the inner world, time might stand still or just disappear; or even do something else in a rather bumpy course.

The reading process needs at least both factual and psychological time. Moreover, time in poetry seems to be rather periodic. So, at least three kinds of time should be relevant when reading poetry:

- *Scientific time* is modelled after the Big Bang and the progressing entropy. The universe becomes invariably colder and colder and the stars move further away from each other to finally burn out. Scientific time moves invariably forward, and this forward direction basically governs all other experiences of time. This is what philosophy uses to name the *Time Arrow* (Hoy 2009).
- *Psychological time* disregards the time arrow and seems to do whatever – rush, halt, or evaporate. One moment might be experienced as if it contained a whole life, while other moments never unfold. Time might be stopped or repeated; it stays in the now. Such a time line does not picture an arrow but rather a knotted rope. Anyone can recognize these peculiarities from the process of grasping a piece of art.[4]
- We may notice that time in nature is strikingly *periodic*. Think of the phases of the moon, day and night following each other, seasons returning year after year, children growing up and taking the place of their parents in society. This *cyclical time* manipulates the forward direction of scientific time by looking more like a spiral than an arrow. The repeated moment – springtime, for example – calls back to its previous occasions. A repetition makes us able to keep the first and the second occasion and all the time in between them present in mind at the same time. Many versification tools intend to periodize time (Tsur's back-structured gestalts, Jakobson's rhyming equivalences).

These different concepts of time work in the reading process. Scientific time firmly moves forward, when experienced time jumps around, halts and moves in spirals. However, the time arrow basically always governs the process. Uniform

---

[4] Narrating changes scientific time to psychological time. The narrative makes meaning (Ricœur [1985] 1990: 129). See also Turner 1996.

time shapes the reading time – a poem needs a certain amount of clock time to be read, or listened to, but also to be understood.

Reading a poem is a mental occurrence that is in need of factual reading time. The scientific and the psychological time aspects behave quite differently even if they cooperate. Reading a poem will take you a couple of factual minutes. In the psychological reading process, however, you will shape that time according to rhythmical construction and semantic information. Focus points are decided, like directions and tempo, and, in this inner world, time has the possibility to stand still if needed (Cureton 1992: 427). The verse line moves forward in factual time but might keep still in the reader's inner time. The poem uses various tricks that aim to manipulate time, hereby borrowing models from a body that moves in a room.[5] Falling rhythm looks back – this is what happens in the Cohen poem in line 11 – and balanced phrases seem to stand still (in l. 1). Two forces are at stake here – clock time that is moving forward, and the attention that is directed backwards or focused on the now.

The biorhythms of the body create a feeling of forwardness that consolidates the factual time arrow (Attridge 2013: 41–5). Other directions – looking back, standing still – complicate this basic situation. They are marked; that is, they deviate from what is expected. Traditionally, a main category within versification studies has been precisely 'direction'. *Rising direction* (oO, ooO, oooO and so on) goes forward along with factual time, and *falling rhythm* (Oo, Ooo, Oooo and so on) seems to leave something and look back, which is most possible in psychological time (Tsur 2017: 50; Kruckenberg and Fant 1993). To these classic forms, I would like to add the category of *standing still*; for example, a molossus OOO or the cretic OoO. This could also be done in psychological time.

*Imagined time* is a kind of psychological time and, as a matter of fact, also an aesthetic category (Ricœur 1990: 129). The reader visualizes what happens in the poem inside himself. In the Cohen poem, I take part in a short story – a situation is pictured, then the girl says something after which the protagonist reacts. It is easy to see that scene in the fantasy. It makes up the time line of a narrative, and all stories are directed forward. What will happen later on, they ask. The reader is waiting for the prolongation goal – in this case the man's reaction (this is the goal of the narrative, which is not to

---

[5] Tsur explains the time drive with a so-called 'limited channel capacity' of the brain. The heaviest element must be the last one so as not to burden the channel capacity. Tsur 2017: 24, 26, 40.

be confused with the prolongation goal of the poem, 'with all her small voice trembling' oOoOOOo).

## Time and repetition

The world rushes to its destruction through cold and darkness (forward), but one experiences the return of spring every year (periodic time). Every human is born and dies (forward), but new babies are born all the time (periodic time). Like a spiral, time moves forward just to return, repeatedly onwards and after that back again (for more about repetition, see Chapter 11).

Repetition means a feedback process that points at some earlier occasion. You return to what is already stated. Time is always heading forward, but turning the attention backwards means a way of going back or standing still. Time becomes cyclic – you are allowed to stay in the moment, which is something that gives you extra room to intensify both thought and feeling. The categorization is delayed; you are given the opportunity to assimilate everything that the moment says to you (Tsur 2008: 185 and others). This extra time will deepen our thinking and expand our feeling which needs time to develop and intensify.

In Chapter 3, I referred to Roman Jakobson's (1960: 358) so-called 'principle of equivalence' which emphasizes all kinds of approximate similarity in poems (even if rhyming is crucial for him). The temporal flow processes repeat signification. Repetition (time) makes similarity (space). Rhyme words are sound repetitions. According to Jakobson, poetry is signified by repeated form elements. Every repetition points back at a previous moment of the text. Reading follows time in a forward manner, of course, but the repetition directs the attention backwards. This will create an experience of going back or standing still. When reading poetry, you are allowed to stay in the moment – the time arrow seems to have stopped its lugubrious way, which intensifies the reading experience (Tsur 2008: 185). The time spiral makes a tense standstill.

Turning back in the text will give the reader the opportunity to expand the moment and keep its meaning intact for many seconds in a sort of eternal now. Time seems to stand still just like a body in balance. The time course seems to stop, which allows the reader to be aware of all the text in between the two repeated expressions – both its form and its significance. The now is expanded.

The Cohen poem of this chapter evidently illustrates such a process. It is very obvious that the forward direction dominates its rhythm – many lines are iambic and the closing row of anapaests underlines its forwardness a little more. However, there is a significant repetition, a reestablishment that connects lines 6–7 to line 11.

...

| | | |
|---|---|---|
| l. 6 | And she said, I for one | o OO / O o O > |
| | am happy with the world | o O ooo O |
| l. 8 | She seized the lapel of a cut-throat | o O o O o / oo O0 |
| | and said it again | o O oo O |
| l. 10 | with all her small voice trembling, | o O o OOO o |
| | I for one am happy with the world | O o O / o O ooo O |

...

In between the repeated phrases, lines 8–10 happen, and these three lines are allowed to stay in an expanded moment, which is something that will highlight their importance. I have said it before – the hot spot of this poem is to be found in line 10, where the molossus gives us the character of the girl, and that way lets us know how the story will end.

# Part 2

# Reading free verse rhythms

# 7

# Cognitive economy

## What is cognitive economy?

In this chapter I will discuss the simplifying process that occurs in the reading, what Tsur calls 'cognitive economy'. When reading a poem, sound patterns change a little on their way to the mind.[1] The reader simplifies and patterns the poetical text into distinct figures, but the same process will be at stake in ordinary speech where strong figures are desired. Often a pair, two of something, is a preferred form, and the ticktock of a clock will show us how this works. Of course, 'tick' and 'tock' are equally strong, but the listener imposes a difference, making the 'tick' a little stronger. When people are speaking in an ordinary manner, they seem to strive for alternation oO oO oO and do not initially choose the spondee OO, which makes it even more expressive when it happens.

I have pointed at this phenomenon many times before – there is a small difference between the acoustic measurements of a verse line with the notation of what one actually hears. And, as Starr and others have stated, thereby recitation and silent reading have the same effect. The registration is objective and the notation subjective. The human notation shows a stronger tendency towards patterning, where objective registration of the sound stream points towards more noise between stresses than is to be heard. Obviously, many sounds are never perceived and, moreover, there is a more evident contrast between prominent syllables and weak ones in what is perceived. The reader reduces unnecessary details and simplifies the pattern (Lilja 2007).

This phenomenon can be explained with the help of some psychology. Gestalt psychology (Chapter 2) has developed into cognitive psychology, where findings

---

[1] Reading a poem aloud creates a temporal sequence of sounds that follow one after the other. Modern poetry, however, is mostly read silently, but even so one hears the sounds of the poem in one's head (Linde 1974: 40; Starr 2013: 91).

in brain research give us new explanations (Chapter 5). Gestalt psychology has taught us that perceptions of the world are mainly apprehended as entireties (Ash 1995; Tsur 2012a: 17). The gestalt laws describe how impressions are reorganized in the perception and this process contains a reductive moment. *Simplicity* is the key term of the gestalt principles of perception (Tsur 2012a: 63), and simple patterns also tend to be strong and independent. The tendency towards simplicity governs the process when patterning the rhythm in verse. The reader will experience this mechanism as a pressure to form distinct gestalts – the so-called 'gestalt pressure'. When reading a poem, gestalt pressure makes one react towards simplicity and efficiency.

Reuven Tsur has adapted gestalt theory to modern cognitive psychology in his versification theory (Tsur 2008). He calls this process of simplification 'cognitive economy' (Tsur 2008: 36–37; Kühl 2007: 89; Neisser 1976). Tsur mostly investigates acoustic registrations of actors' interpretations of classical texts in Milton and Shakespeare, and he has noticed that the reader tends to transform the poetic text into stronger and more distinct gestalts than the printed text really offers. A reduction in the cognitive process will take over and simplify the rhythmic patterns. Such an articulation saves mental space in a process of so-called mental economy.

What Tsur calls cognitive economy changes natural pronunciation, thereby making patterns simpler (Tsur 2012a: ch. 2). It increases the contrast between what is strong and what is weak, which is especially obvious in cadenced versification. Unconsciously, the reader will choose the most efficient form; that which is most convenient to process. A distinct pattern is simply economical and uses less space in the brain (Tsur 2012a: 295).

As I have already noted, the short-term memory is limited, about three seconds in length (Tsur 2008: 172–3; Pöppel 2004). This is also the time span of an ordinary verse line that uses around ten to eleven syllables – like a common pentameter line but also a very usual span in the medieval four-beat line and in modern free verse. To be used effectively, this interval must be grouped and articulated (Tsur 2008: 8, 167). One will save mental space when grouping sound impulses into strong and simple figures. Tactus is the most obvious example of cognitive economy, of simplifying sound impulses in order to be maximally easy to process, but free verse may also present strong and salient patterns.

However, from this will follow that weak gestalts and divergent formal devices allow more sounds to be pronounced and perceived (Tsur 2008: 92). This will influence the signification process. What kinds of significance will be revealed from strong and weak gestalts, respectively? T.S. Eliot's 'Ash Wednesday' (1930) consists of strong as well as weak gestalts as I will show in examples from two stanzas.

## T.S. Eliot's 'Ash Wednesday'

Early free verse may be classified according to the origin of its form elements (see the Introduction, pp. 7–8). Old German free verse emanated from Greek colon versification, where spondee and enjambment are significant traits (Hellmuth 1973: 252). The expressionists preferred this type of free verse. German free verse by Heinrich Heine took its form elements from medieval forms like the chronicle and the ballad; this is the four-beat line made of stylized speech phrases (Lilja 2003). The Anglo-American imagists preferred this simpler type of free verse, and T.S. Eliot connected to this school.

Eliot commented on the new free versification in an essay called 'Reflections on Vers Libre' in *New Statesman* (1917). 'No verse is free', he says – a sentence that has received various interpretations for more than a century (cf. Hrushovski 1960: 176). Eliot also commented on free versification in his essay 'The Music in Poetry' (1942). He promotes the idea of a tight relationship between form and content, which should be unique for every single poem. This is the standard motivation in early modernism for using free verse. When discussing how to structure a poem, Eliot makes music analogies. In *Four Quartets* (1943), Eliot was inspired by the structures of the sonata. His techniques of repetition refer to music as well; for example, parallelisms and paronomasias. End-stopped lines dominate in his poems and enjambments are exceptions.

Eliot's so-called conversational style is especially interesting from a rhythmical point of view. He points out that ordinary speech – the language of conversation – is the most important field of study for exploring the rhythm of free verse (Eliot [1942] 1958). In his writing, he cultivates tendencies of common English speech. Some typical phrase patterns appear because of certain traits in English syntax like constructions with 'of', such as *The Heart of Darkness* o O o O o – the most frequent phrase pattern in *Four Quartets*. This pattern is, of course, just as frequent in ordinary English speech. Eliot borrows such tendencies in speech and styles them into something more salient (Finch 1993: 87). As already stated, the medieval four-beat line comes close to a natural speech rhythm and, of course, this is the same case with the imagist type of free verse.

Eliot wrote his essay 'Reflections on Vers Libre' as early as 1917, now more than a century ago; much has happened within the field of versification since then. Of course, his own verse technique changed over time. A freely used four-beat line is its most significant device, but other patterns are to be found. 'The Love Song of J. Alfred Prufrock' (1917) uses a loosely handled pentameter. Parts of 'The Waste Land' (1922) have a four-beat line as a basic pattern and other parts have the pentameter. The very first page of this famous poem with its heavy enjambments comes close to antique versification. In *Four Quartets* (1943), the four-beat line is a dominating influence, and so on (Cooper 1998: 43–66).

'Ash Wednesday' consists of six poems. The excerpts below are a part of the first poem, stanza 3 and 4. Several types of free verse are at stake in these two stanzas. I will compare them in relation to how, in the sense of Tsur, economic they are, and how the degree of economy influences signification.

```
      ...
      Because I know that time is always time
 2    And place is always and only place
      And what is actual is actual only for one time
 4    And only for one place
      I rejoice that things are as they are and
 6    I renounce the blessed face
      And renounce the voice
 8    Because I cannot hope to turn again
      Consequently I rejoice, having to construct something
10    Upon which to rejoice
                              ('Ash Wednesday' I (1930) stanza 3)
```

And the fourth stanza continues:

```
      And pray to God to have mercy upon us
 2    And I pray that I may forget
      These matters that with myself I too much discuss
 4    Too much explain
      Because I do not hope to turn again
 6    Let these words answer
```

For what is done, not to be done again
8   May the judgement not be too heavy upon us
    …
                              ('Ash Wednesday' I (1930) stanza 4)

Some lines here have a subtle pentameter, and some are written in the four-beat pattern. Others are shaped with the help of spondaic figures (the antique type of free verse), still others are weak gestalts.[2] I will show the complexity of Eliot's verse, and point at how free verse of different types work together.

| | | | stresses |
|---|---|---|---|
| Stanza 3: | | | |
| | o O o O / o O o O o O | pentameter | 5 |
| 3:2 | o O o O o / o O o O > | four-beat line | 4 |
| | o O o O o / o O o O o / o O O | spondee | 6 |
| 3:4 | o O o / o O O | spondee | 3 |
| | oo O o O / O oo O O > | spondee | 4(5) |
| 3:6 | oo O / o O O | spondee | 3 |
| | oo O o O | | 2 |
| 3:8 | o O o O o O / o O o O | pentameter | 5 |
| | O o 0 ooo O/O ooo OO o | spondee, weak | 6 OoooooOooooOOo |
| 3:10 | oo O oo O | anapaests | 2 |
| Stanza 4: | | | |
| | o O o O / oo O oo O o | four-beat line | 4 |
| 4:2 | oo O / oo O o O > | | 3 |
| | O O o / ooo O / o OO o O | 2 spondees, weak | 6(4) |
| 4:4 | O O o O | weak | 3 oOoO |
| | o O o O o O / o O o O | pentameter | 5 |
| 4:6 | o O O O o | molossus | 3 |
| | o O o O/O oo O o O | pentameter | 5 oOoOoOoOoO |
| 4:8 | oo O o / oo O O oo O o | four-beat line | 4 ooOo/OooOooOo |

I have observed four kinds of rhythm in these two stanzas: pentameter, the four-beat line, spondaic lines or the antique type of free verse, and what here will be named weak figures. The five beats of a pentameter are to be heard in lines 3:1, 3:8, 4:5 and 4:7, where line 4:5 is a repetition of line 3:8. These lines follow the rule smoothly, they are divided with a caesura in the right places and they run flexibly – like an English pentameter mostly does (in Swedish, for example, with its sharper accents, the pentameter works more heavily, and is not often practised). As a whole, an end-stopped English pentameter line makes a strong pattern.

---

[2] Many commentators have thought that 'Ash Wednesday' is written in pentameter (Jansson 1991: 142). However, the notation shows that this only concerns some of the lines.

The four-beat line is practised in lines 3:2, 4:1 and 4:8. This measure also needs a caesura, which is something that is to be found in these three lines. Line 4:8 has a small deviation from the rule, when only one of the four stresses is situated in the first half line. The second half line of line 4:8 can be interpreted in two ways: with the second stress on the fifth syllable, or on the seventh. Both these readings are good, and one may choose according to taste. The four-beat line is not a cadenced measure; normally it does not use tactus. However, it is a strong traditional pattern that is spontaneously recognized by everyone in northern Europe and the English-speaking world. If you were to ask school children to write a little poem, they would probably produce a four-beat four-liner (this experiment has been performed).

The third category of lines is signified by its spondees, a characteristic of ancient Greek poetry that became typical of the oldest kind of free verse that was created by Klopstock and Goethe in the eighteenth century (Hellmuth 1973). This type of free verse has grown into something solemn and emphatic. The spondees slow down the tempo and give weight to the text. The excerpt is generous with this ancient device, as it will be found in lines 3:3, 3:4, 3:5, 3:6, 3:9, 4:3 (twice), and 4:6 where it has expanded to a molossus OOO. The repeated spondees in the line endings 3:3–6 keep this passage together like an end rhyme.

Of course, the four-beat line will also contain spondees. As already mentioned, this may be the case in line 4:8. Line 3:5 can be read as a four-beat line if one neglects the special enjambment pronunciation with extra length on the last syllable before the break. But this medieval measure will not bear enjambments.

I have now specified three patterns in this text: the pentameter, the four-beat line and the ancient type of free verse. All of them make strong patterns when simplifying the sound stream, but they do so in different ways. Because of tactus the pentameter works as a strong pattern within the principle of cognitive economy. The four-beat lines do just the same because of cultural habits. Even if the tactus is lacking, this four-beat pattern dominates Germanic-speaking minds, and it is easy to interpret such lines.

The spondaic free verse will also make strong figures, but requires some more effort. In line 3:3–4 the finishing repeated spondees organize the preceding pattern of oOoOo (shortened in l. 3:4). These lines are very end-stopped:

l. 3:3  And what is actual is actual only for one time    o O o O o / o O o O o / o O O
       And only for one place    o O o / o O O

Many words are repeated here, which also brings repeated rhythm patterns with them. Repetition is, among other things, a device that strengthens the gestalt.

The molossus of line 4:6, 'Let these words answer' o OOO o, breaks the soft alternating sequences of the preceding lines, making it forceful – as already said, three stresses in a row take extra energy to pronounce.[3] This is a strong pattern but not an economical one. Evidently, strong gestalts are not always comfortable or economical. A pentameter needs less energy than a four-beat line, which nonetheless is such a deep cultural pattern that the native reader will immediately recognize it. The spondaic free verse lines are strong figures insofar as they use two unquestionable stresses – like 'one time' OO in line 3:3. By contrast, 'Too much' OO in line 4:4 is a preferred reading that is possible to change (oO); because of this it is not a strong gestalt. But are the spondaic lines economical?

Weak gestalts are signified by an uncertainty about how to read them. Several possibilities for organizing the stresses are at stake. In these excerpts, line 3:9 and line 4:3 must be defined as weak figures. Here, one must also consider the lines that frame them – the pentameter of line 3:8, and the four-beat pattern of line 4:1. Some other lines could be performed with a slightly mixed tactus – there are two anapaests in line 3:10, and anapaests also in line 4:2. Line 4:4, here notated as the third epitrite OOoO, may also be understood as a double iamb oOoO – if one is looking for alternating patterns. The two possibilities also make this line a weak gestalt.

|      | ... | |
|------|------------------------------------|------------------------|
| 3:8  | Because I cannot hope to turn again | o O o O o O / o O o O |
|      | Consequently I rejoice, having<br>    to construct something | O ooooo O/O ooo OO o |
| 3:10 | Upon which to rejoice | oo O oo O |
|      | And pray to God to have mercy upon us | o O o O / oo O oo O o |
| 4:2  | And I pray that I may forget | oo O / oo O o O > |
|      | These matters that with myself<br>    I too much discuss | O O o / ooo O / o OO o O |
| 4:4  | Too much explain | O O o O |
|      | ... | |

---

[3] It would be possible to read this molossus with varied pronunciations of the three stresses (Tsur 2012a: 143). If one chooses length for the first stress 'these', pitch for the second one 'words' and again length for the third one 'answer', the alternation will somehow be kept alive.

I have understood the first phrase in line 3:9 to have two stresses and five weak syllables that are organized in a so-called 'cot' – stresses are situated at the very start and the very end in the phrase, with the weaks hanging between them. The second half line moves, in my interpretation, much in the same way with another row of weaks before the final spondee that stops the rush, 'construct something' oOOo (antispast). It would also be possible to read line 3:9 as a big and loose four-beat line OooooooO/ooooOOo. Here are other possible alternative interpretations – the third syllable of the line might have secondary stress (notated with a 0) and the first syllable of the second half line could be unstressed Oo0oooO/ooooOOo.[4] It is also possible to read the line with a slight alternation up to the spondee, but here I would dispute that conversational style prefers many weaks. This line makes a weak figure because of the uncertainties, and because of the number of weak syllables that are in combination with the determining spondee that stops inclinations to possibly read it in an alternating manner.

Turning to the second weak line, line 4:3, there are different possibilities as well. I have chosen to realize two spondees as well as a rising paeon oooO in three phrases of six stresses together, but another interpretation would be a four-beat line:

l. 4:3   These matters that with myself I too much discuss      oOooooOooOoO

However, as a four-beat line, this one seems too big and loose, and too difficult to pronounce (lines with this somewhat ponderous shape are common; for example, in the chronicles of the fifteenth century). Even with that kind of reading, line 4:3 would be a weak gestalt with uncertain pronunciations that offer several possibilities, and the repeated epitrite OO o O of line 4:4 supports the spondaic interpretation in the end of line 4:3.

|   | / I too much discuss | o OO o O |
|---|---|---|
| l. 4:4 | Too much explain | OO o O |

I started this discussion by saying that tactus is the most obvious example of cognitive economy and of simplifying sound impulses in order to make them maximally easy to handle. But the four-beat line also takes advantage of cognitive economy. Free verse presents strong and salient patterns, but they are perhaps not that economical. In these excerpts there are strong free verse gestalts as well

---

[4] In the section 'How to read free verse', pp. 11–13. I remarked that a row of many weaks may indicate that a place for rest, an extra stress, is being sought. A possible syllable to rest upon in l. 3:9:1 might be the 'I'.

as very loose ones. Eliot's free verse, in these excerpts, offers gestalts of more or less weakness. Some passages make one hesitate – the rhythmical elements allow different directions, which give extra room for personal understanding. The slow categorization, that is the consequence of the ambiguities, creates time to increase emotion.[5] This was an obvious purpose of the free verse pioneers a century ago – to slow down the reading and, that way, force the poem to draw close to the reader, as many poets say in their famous manifestos.

Throughout these texts, there is an interaction between a dim alternation and strong spondees that break the flow and tell the reader that this is modern free verse.

## Signification

The reduction process, as discussed in this chapter, differentiates the possibilities of signification. Weak and uneconomical forms may add more information and more emotion than economical ones. Weak forms support difficult feelings and complicated thoughts. Strong patterns, by contrast, produce distinct signification – form and meaning cooperate into something clear and evident (Tsur 2008: 59–61). This is certainly true, but I would like to remonstrate that the connections between form and significance might be more complicated.

Poetic language is distinguished by deautomatization, with form elements that break through the automated speech language (Tynyanov [1924] 1981: 26, 47, 62; Kristeva [1974] 1984: 86–88). Ordinary speech does not allow us to hear its acoustic parts – the speech process is automated – but poetry activates the right as well as the left half of the brain (Tsur 2017: 40). Like music (right side), poetry concentrates on form and feeling, and like dissertations (left side) it delivers rather complicated thoughts. A reader must be attentive.

The reduction process of cognitive economy may increase the information of a line, making it structured and lucid, but at the same time significance is reduced as some sounds are lost. Here Tsur's example is Alexander Pope's poetry, clear and intellectual (e.g. Tsur 2008: 141). Strong phrases may transfer clear thoughts, but I would say, also strong feelings like uncomplicated rage. An angry person tends towards a cadenced expression, and the more infuriated the person

---

[5] Compare with Tsur's concept of divergency (2008: 185).

is, the stronger the tactus. A hard seriality will take over the dictum, and the form becomes most forceful. The angry person gets very explicit without any nuances (Mannerheim 1991: 171).

Yet another example of emotion-generating tactus refers to a clergyman delivering his sermon. I listened to him in a small church in northern Gothenburg about twenty years ago. While talking, he got more and more exalted and at a certain moment he swished over to a steady seriality. His prose suddenly turned to a heavy metre. The clergyman seemed to be hypnotized by his own voice.

An angry man gains in force when he delivers his arguments in cadences, but this was not the case with the sermon. I would say that, when cadenced, it lost its intellectual quality and became difficult to understand. Obviously, this clergyman was most engaged in his subject, but the message became rather hidden. I conclude that the relationship between an economical form and lucid content is complex (cf. Tsur 2003; Snyder 1930).

But also the weak figures of Eliot's poem relate to significance. Form elements can be read in different ways, and slow categorization creates time to acquire the text deeply. When struggling for textual sense, the reader's own experiences may be given room in the poem. If strong, economical figures reduce the amount of sound slipping through into consciousness, the weak figures allow more sounds to be heard at the cost, maybe, of some confusion.

Also, regarding weak figures, facts provide a complex picture. Marianne Nordman (1987) has investigated various kinds of non-literary prose. She found that handbooks and manuals of different kinds are most divergent according to language rhythm. The language of bureaucracy seems to be extremely uneconomical as it is trying to avoid being emotional. Official papers concentrate on content with no interest in a salient form – before anything else, they will reduce any possibility for misunderstandings. The Swedish texts at stake in Nordman's investigation produce many secondary stresses, often in combination with stresses O0, O00 and cumulated weak syllables ooooo. Often such dictums are felt to be rhythmically unstructured. Bureaucratic language exemplifies weak figures that have no emotional qualities. Eliot's weak figures indicate how to handle signification in uneconomical lines. But first a strong figure:

l. 4:6  Let these words answer         o OOO o

Line 4:6 makes a strong figure but needs some effort to read – it is not easy going, which is something that emphasizes its weightiness. This gestalt is simultaneously strong and in need of extra attention.

l. 3:9 Consequently I rejoice, having to construct something
...
l. 4:3 These matters that with myself I too much discuss

l. 3:9  O o 0 ooo O/O ooo OO o    or    OoooooO/ooooOOo
...
l. 4:3  OO o / ooo O / o OO o O

Above I have discussed various possibilities of how to read these two weak lines, and every interpretation gives room for new significances. If, in line 3:9, one takes advantage of the possibility of two stresses in 'Consequently', it will give extra weight to this word. If playing it down, not caring for the idea of a cause in this passage, but more eager to stress the repeated weak rows of the line, the connection between 'rejoice' and 'construct' will be emphasized. My (unnecessary) stress on 'hav[ing]' points out the same connection.

In my notation of line 4:3, there are two spondees, in the beginning and in the end of the line. This way, 'These' and 'too' are given extra weight, the line will have six prominences and the relationship to the four-beat pattern will be lost. Read in this way, the line is understood to be one of the most important in this excerpt. The extra stresses emphasize the discussed matter of the line and cooperate with the molossus of line 4.6, which is also heavy in signification. Thereby, I have reduced the syllable stress ratio from 3 down to a harmonized 2 – half the syllables are prominences just as in an ideal pentameter.

## Strong and weak gestalts

I have distinguished some possibilities according to strong and weak patterns. Strong patterns may be distinct – this is not only true in content but also in feeling. However, strong reduction may also lead to a kind of hypnosis. Weak figures may leave room for interesting thoughts and feelings, but they may also be somewhat bland.

A good poem mixes different kinds of figures, strong and weak patterns cooperate well, and the mingling itself creates quality.

I have also found a possibility that has previously not been mentioned. Antique free verse makes strong figures, but the cognitive economic reduction does not work in this case. They break through in the stream of speech, and they are often given the mission of carrying the most important thoughts of the poem.

# 8

# The poem in the body

## Bodily experiences

This chapter investigates how biorhythms relate to verse rhythm. As already mentioned in the Introduction, Plato describes the rhythm of a dancing body in terms of 'organized movement'. Motion seems to be the very core of the rhythmic experience, as stated in, for example, Attridge's *Moving Words* (2013) and in Cureton, who stresses a rhythmical motion in time as the main quality of versification (1992). A limited movement seems to be the base of any aesthetic rhythm, and rhythm in poetry could be understood as patterns of motion within gestalts.

This observation has been highlighted by recent neurological studies (Starr 2013: ch. 2). The motor systems of the brain are crucial to perceptual and imagined experiences. Motor imagery can be produced even when motion is not represented – like in music or static pictures. The complex, distributed motor systems in the brain underpin phenomena of embodiment, like the aesthetic experience in the body (Starr 2013: 83–4). Imagined movements integrate with various kinds of perceptions and modalities.[1] As for music, bodies move in accordance with the tactus. As for pictures, motions are constructed out of expectations – there is an interpenetration of sight and motion, as visual images use brain areas that are normally used for planning our own motions (Starr 2013: 85–6, 99).

The human body is rhythmic. One needs only to think of heart beats, breathing and, not least, walking. In this perspective, the experience of rhythms

---

[1] Motor imagery should be understood as imagined movements (Starr 2013: 91–2, 99). Starr also discusses which mechanisms are at work in an aesthetic experience (2013: 24): Perceptions and meaning emanate from sensations/imagery and memory/emotion. Brain centres active in this process are sensory cortex, basal ganglia, hippocampus, amygdala, and orbitofrontal cortex. They produce complex processes of cognition, emotion and reward.

seems to emanate out of the reality of the body. Aesthetic rhythms, in the first step, seem to be formed in accordance with human biorhythms such as walking, dancing, pulse, sex and breathing. In the next step, they are processed by culture, environment and tradition. The perceived world and the person are mutually defined through both bodily and cultural experience (Varela, Thompson, and Rosch 1993: 172; Sonesson 2007: 110–11).

If the motor systems of the brain influence perceptions in all kinds of modalities, the experience of movement in a poem is more than a metaphor. A poem can be likened to a body (Hopsch and Lilja 2017). It could also be argued that the poem, like a sculpture, has a visible body – taking the form of print, letters and paper. When listening to a poem, there is also an acoustic body to enjoy. Furthermore, the body of the poem is shaped through 'the cognitive processes by which a literary work is created and understood. Understanding is embodied, … signification, imagination, and reasoning have a physical basis in our experience of the world' (Freeman 2002: 43). Perceiving rhythm (and everything else) presupposes a neurological base – one can only grasp what the brain allows us. What is rhythm, relies on a cognitive steering system referring to motor skills, language, gestalts and perception schemas that are conscious as well as subconscious.[2]

Rhythm in poetry also crucially depends on the speech organs. The science of phonetics describes them thoroughly. The character of speech sounds is due to the form of the tongue, teeth and palate. Speech also relies on breathing, and I will return to that later.

The experience of being a body that is influenced by gravity with the ability to walk as well as dance is basic for everyone. The experiences of our bodies also determine how to comprehend things like truth and reason. What I think to be true must of course depend on how to understand the situation; this in turn depends on perceptions and motor impulses (Lakoff and Johnson 1999: 106–8). The key concept here is experience. Even reason depends on bodily experience, because basic abilities to think descend from body-based forms of inference. A one-year-old learning to walk instinctively follows Euclid's axiom that the shortest ways between two points is a straight line.

---

[2] Compare with Lakoff and Johnson's idea of a cognitive subconscious (1999: 116).

## Intervals

The biorhythms that underlie aesthetic rhythms affect the sensory impulses of versification. The motor schemas occur at the levels of line and phrase. For example, the tactus of a poem might be based in the human experience of heart beat, or the steps of walking, and sequences of free verse might be formed out of motor schemas like leaping and running – or resting. The human body really does look like a system of wider and smaller rhythms. Hormones and neurons all dance in rhythmical patterns. One cannot judge their exact relations to poetry, at least not yet, but the following rhythms are more than likely involved:

- The echo memory with an interval of about half a second is most evidently recognized in cadenced poetry – the interval between prominences mostly endures about half a second. This is serial rhythm that is to be found, for example, in the pattern of iambic pentameter. Moreover, serial rhythm is practised by the walking body when taking one step after another. Also, the pulse seems to have something to do with the serial rhythm of metered versification.
- The three (or more precisely, two to five) seconds of the short-term memory cover approximately a normal line length and a breath. The sequential rhythm dominates modern free verse as well as the medieval four-beat line, and of course the musical phrase. The three-second interval of a common verse line and the short-term memory coincides, approximately, with the breath interval.
- Long-term memory uses more than three seconds. In the poem it offers rhythmic patterns out of, among other things, sensorimotor experiences – like walking, with its many possibilities. Dynamic rhythm needs some more time than an iamb or a line.

These three time levels of embodiment coincide with the three principles of rhythm that are described in Chapter 1: serial, sequential and dynamic rhythm – the three basic sets of gestalt qualities. They coincide as well with Figure 5.4 in Chapter 5 (p. 73) that analyses the development from sound to signification. The time span of about 0.5 second returns in the serial principle of rhythm and the precategorial position of the perception process. The, approximately, three seconds level is interesting for sequential rhythm as well as for premodal patterning (second column). Concerning long-term memory, dynamic prolongations and meaning construction need more than three seconds (third column).

Pöppel and Turner (Turner and Pöppel 1983; Pöppel 2004; Trevarthen 2009) discovered that the span of short-term memory of three seconds coincides with the span of common verse lines. This is a universal interval in poetry from different cultures. The extension of the short-term memory seems to determine the length of a normal verse line – 10 to 11 syllables – all over the world.[3] Their discovery explains the most typical device of poetry – the division into short lines. That which is possible to keep in mind at the same time is surrounded by the limits of line breaks, small pauses of about half a second. This device pictures poetry as a string of expressive moments – unlike prose that is continuous. Turner and Pöppel's results suppose a kind of digital reading of poetry: the reader keeps all meaning of the line in mind simultaneously, and with the line break it is pushed into the long-term memory, and s/he prepares for a new moment. Prose, however, works analogously by continuously spreading out signification. Such a digital reading might explain some of the magic of poetry.

Pöppel has continued to confirm his findings with further investigations. Other researchers have supported him, like Manfred Spitzer in Ulm, who is a neurologist as well as a musician (Spitzer 2002). Spitzer's results in neurology for aesthetic use also support theories of Reuven Tsur and Mark Johnson. The basic concept of gestalt could be understood in the light of human brain memories and their characteristics.

The poet plays with all these time limits. Of course, there are verse lines of all sizes, from one syllable to several lines. But a line that is shorter than the 'normal' of about ten syllables is felt to be a short line, and one that exceeds that size seems to be a long one. Again, an ordinary speech phrase mostly consists of two prominences and three to four weak syllables. Often two such speech phrases form one intonation phrase, and one verse line of average size. A speech phrase makes a possible half line in a four-beat line or in a pentameter with their size of about ten syllables. However, the poem of this chapter, Seamus Heaney's 'Sloe Gin', also plays games with that possible norm.

---

[3] For the sake of Europe, the *hendekasillaba* (or eleven syllables) has dominated. Most classical metres were established during the late Middle Age in the Romance countries. They were mostly founded upon a line of eleven syllables. Later on, the Germanic cultures developed iambic pentameter out of the *hendekasillaba* combined with the domestic rhythms of the four-beat line.

The half second interval has also been important. In versification studies, pulse and heart beats have been favourite subjects. Of course, this is due to another favourite – the tactus. Cadenced poetry from earlier times mostly used serial rhythm – rhythms connected with regular biorhythms. A lingering reading of cadenced poetry – and poems should be read in a relatively slow tempo – will make about one stress every half second, which is the same interval that is used for hypnosis (Snyder 1930; Tsur 2003). This interval comes close to the pulse as well as step and echo memory. Magicians and shamans always know this when invoking the spirits or throwing their audiences into a trance.

The beating heart has also interested psychologists. The foetus listens to the beating heart of the mother, which is why regular rhythms ease a crying baby. Regular rhythms invoke safe and pleasurable feelings. Regular heart beats mean life, while irregular ones signify danger. So far, versification studies have not explored sexual rhythms which may also affect the text.

All these intervals are approximate. The short-term memory lasts for three seconds, or, it would be between two and five seconds. Its capacity is, to a certain degree, negotiable – it is possible to put a strain on it by grouping or to diminish it by irregularities. The same should be the case with the echo memory. A measured biorhythm will not be perfectly regular, but the experienced rhythm, that is the cadenced gestalt, can be most stated. As demonstrated in Chapter 7, the reader generates this evenness himself.

In this chapter, I have compared certain versification spans with some bodily rhythms. Long-term memory offers rhythm patterns that are either cultural, or cognitive out of biorhythms or iconicity. I have investigated embodied patterns – experiences like pulse, breathing and walking, which shape neurological schemas and order sound impulses (Spitzer 2002: 227). One may remember that a step lasts for about half a second, but the biorhythm of walking needs more time, which exceeds the interval of three seconds. The walking body appears to be a model for rhythmic patterning.

## A moving poem

One level of reading Seamus Heaney's poem 'Sloe Gin' depends essentially on bodily knowledge. However, cultural devices also influence the rhythm. It is a realistic description around a central image that describes how to brew sloe schnapps in a rural household and later on, when winter has arrived, the pleasure of tasting it.

|  |  |  | Stresses | Syllables |
|---|---|---|---|---|
|  | The clear weather of juniper | o OO o o O oo | 3 | 9 |
| 2 | darkened into winter. | O ooo O o | 2 | 6 |
|  | She fed gin to sloes | o 0O o O | 2 or 3 | 5 |
| 4 | and sealed the glass container. | o O o O o O o | 3 | 7 |
|  | When I unscrewed it | o 0 oO o | 1 or 2 | 5 |
| 6 | I smelled the disturbed | o O oo O > | 2 | 5 |
|  | tart stillness of a bush | OO ooo O | 3 | 6 |
| 8 | rising through the pantry. | O ooo O o | 2 | 6 |
|  | When I poured it | oo O o | 1 | 4 |
| 10 | it had a cutting edge | ooo O o O | 2 | 6 |
|  | and flamed | o O | 1 | 2 |
| 12 | like Betelgeuse. | o O o 0 | 1 or 2 | 4 |
|  | I drink to you | o O o O | 2 | 4 |
| 14 | in smoke-mirled, blue- | o OO / O > | 3 | 4 |
|  | black sloes, bitter | OO / O o > | 3 | 4 |
| 16 | and dependable. | oo O oo | 1 | 5 |

(Seamus Heaney, 'Sloe Gin', *Station Island*, 1984)

At a first glance, the versification of the poem seems to be traditional, using the four-line stanza. At the same time, its phrase rhythm is free and modern. The speech rhythm here reminds us of the medieval four-beat line, but in this case the lines are shorter – with only one to three stresses. It comes close to ordinary speech, when using zero to three unstressed syllables between stresses. Also, the four-line stanza connects this poem to the medieval ballad. One might say that Heaney mixes modernist free rhythms with some devices from old popular forms.

When reading 'Sloe Gin', I have chosen to follow walking rhythms like rushing, jumping and stopping. But, of course, many other body rhythms can be traced in a poem like this. Alternation calls for the pulse – the time span of half a second (l. 4–5 and l. 8–13). The time limit of an ordinary verse line with about ten syllables is broken – the lines of 'Sloe Gin' are much shorter, and this discrepancy makes the rhythm easy-going.

This poem lives through its exquisite sensory impressions and its dominating image, the drink. The 'I' of the poem speaks to a 'you', who may be taken as the reader. It mixes light-footed alternation with two very heavy parts – there is a soft forward movement that is broken twice by stamping and standing molossi OOO. Stanzas 1 and 3 are dominated by an easy-going alternation that comes close to ordinary speech, as well as walking. Stanzas 2 and 4, however, are heavier. An anticipation rises up to an axis, a concentration of stresses, and after that there is a fading out in extensions. Or, this poem mostly toddles off but it stops twice in a determined balance – an experience that might be easily recognized from our own bodies.

Stanza 1–2:   alternation + anticipation-axis/molossus-extension
Stanza 3–4:         "              "               "              "

Consider line 3–4:

|      | She fed gin to sloes        | o oO o O        |
|------|----------------------------|-----------------|
| l. 4 | and sealed the glass container. | o O o O o O o |

The latter line consists of three iambs oO, and line 3 is also rising in direction. Motion goes forward in these two lines and comes close to a walking rhythm – there are courses of words and courses of steps, and the time span, of half a second, is about the same for an iamb and for the completed step. Walking could be said to pattern this part of the poem (l. 3–5). Human beings normally walk every day to an extent that turns walking into a dominating pattern of experience that shapes our understanding of the world (Varela, Thompson and Rosch 1993: 172–3). Here, the easy-minded tramping comes to an end with the enjambment in line 6:

|      | When I unscrewed it         | o O o O o     |
|------|-----------------------------|---------------|
| l. 6 | I smelled the disturbed     | o O oo O >    |
|      | tart stillness of a bush    | OO ooo O      |
| l. 8 | rising through the pantry.  | O ooo O o     |

This stanza makes a rather stable rhythm in only one sentence. One intonation curve keeps it together in one acoustic body. In lines 6–7, the previous alternation is broken. These two lines are connected with the help of an enjambment, and the latter starts with a spondee OO that completes the stress at the end of line 6. Together they form a heavy molossus OOO as the enjambment eliminates the line-break pause. The part with these three stresses in the middle of the stanza (O>OO) is the emphasized part, or prolongation goal; what comes before it will be perceived as an anticipation and what follows as an extension (Cureton

1992: 146–53). This composition, however, can only be understood once you have completed the whole form of the stanza – it is back structured (Tsur 2012a: 302–3). The gestalt must be closed before it can be fully perceived and before the temporal lapse can be spatialized. The very first expression of the poem, 'The clear weather' o OO o (l. 1), presents a spondee OO that hints at what is to come in stanzas 2 and 4.

With line 9, the same course starts again – at first, alternation dominates through the following lines until the last, very heavy stanza. The small iambic steps of stanza 3 describe the satisfaction of the 'I', when looking at the result of his brewing:

|  |  |  |
|---|---|---|
|  | When I poured it | oo O o |
| l. 10 | it had a cutting edge | ooo O o O |
|  | and flamed | o O |
| l. 12 | like Betelgeuse. | o O o 0 |

We are told about the beauty of the drink, and the rhythm is most particular – short lines, few stresses and a directed climax in lines 11–12. Cultural traditions supply knowledge about housekeeping and drinking habits. The form also suggests signification of other kinds, such as feeling and attitude. In this stanza, rhythm is even, concentrated and rising. It moves in springy steps with a quality of pure joy – the pleasure of life and beauty, and tasty drinks. There is a tickling contrast between the rural environment and the exquisite quality of both the rhythm and the metaphor of the flaming dark red star.

Like stanza 2, the last stanza of the Heaney poem is very rhythmically balanced. It begins with two iambs oO oO in line 13, but continues with an extreme number of stresses in the next pair of lines:

|  |  |  |
|---|---|---|
|  | I drink to you | o O o O |
| l. 14 | in smoke-mirled, blue- > | o OO / O > |
|  | black sloes, bitter > | OO / O o |
| l. 16 | and dependable. | oo O oo |

Lines 14–15 are connected with another enjambment, and, if one doesn't consider the small pauses, one may note them as follows: o OOOOOO o. So many stresses in a row are clearly against the speech rhythm that otherwise characterizes most of the poem. The same passage also contains alliterations and assonances to a degree that sorts it out: 'smoke' – 'sloes', 'blue' – 'black' – 'bitter'. Like stanza 2, this stanza is balanced by a very heavy axis and a light anticipation as well as extension. Line 16 balances just like lines 14–15. This is the very end

of the poem and it also means closure. Resting at the description of the drink, this double molossus (OOO OOO) produces a broken mood and connects with another ambiguous passage, the tart smell of lines 6–7.

The very last line (l. 16) is very light. Of its five syllables only one is stressed, '-pend', meaning hanging or falling. In the parallel position of line 8, there is an opposite direction, 'rising'. In this way, 'dependable' closes the balance of the whole poem.[4]

So far I have made use of the 0.5-second level and the long-term memory level of the stanza and its entirety when reading this poem. The three-second level here works as a kind of empty pattern. As already said, the lines of 'Sloe Gin' are shorter than average, as shown above beside the notation (p. 106). The normal line length of three seconds is absent – the lengths consist of four to five syllables, or one to three stresses instead of the more normal three to five stresses. In such cases, the poet works with line pairs many times – two short lines together make a normal size. Something like this is to be found in the first stanza. The other three stanzas, however, do not use that easy solution. They keep together as entireties, with a marked pause between them. Thereby, the three-second interval is manipulated from both sides – too short per line and too long for a stanza. These discrepancies add an exquisite rhythm.

## Dancing and walking

Dancing and walking are two ways to move the body. Plato started the rhythm discussion pointing at the ordered movement of dance. Myself, I have pointed at walking as a basic producer of experienced rhythm. The motor schemas have probably developed out of sensorimotor experience (Johnson 1987: 41; Spitzer 2002). The human body works according to a great many rhythms, but I would suggest that patterns of walking and dancing are the most important for aesthetic rhythm (Andrews 2017: 71–86). Reading a poem has been understood as walking along a path (Kjørup 2008). Of course, one might walk slower or faster, or might produce short regular steps of half a second or dancing irregular jumps – like Carmen's dance in Figure 8.1.

Walking and dancing are two ways of moving. They differ according to the two lines I have tried to develop through this text, one of forward motion and the

---

[4] Margaret Freeman made this observation, personal communication.

**Figure 8.1** Dancing can be irregular jumps. 2012. Photo © Nobu Yamamoto.

other a balanced standing still. One kind of movement creates beautiful patterns but rests in the same place. The other kind of movement has a forward drive.

Walking has qualities that are important for aesthetic rhythm – it may be conscious as well as automated. It can be regular, have different tempi, or it could be broken by a leap. Semantically, walking has been considered as a kind of basic movement (Pourcel 2010). Walking can be as serial as heart beats with one important difference – it is possible to decide whether to perform one, but not the other. The pulse continues independently of the person's intention, but the walker may hop or stop if s/he wants to.

The connection with the body makes it easy for us to understand how rhythm can deliver significance to an art work. When dancing and leaping, one is happy but, when full of sorrow, one can hardly move or breathe. However, the tense standing still of balance is full of energy. Compare with the tightrope walker at page 10!

The baby fights to rise to its feet in an absolute desire to walk. This experience is basic for everyone and is filled with significance. It conveys knowledge about strength and velocity, intentions and (lack of) control. Moreover, the walker is able to change destination, and there will be obstacles or turnouts that tempt us towards illogical detours. However, every road has a beginning and an end, so it makes a dominating perception schema (Lakoff and Johnson 1999: 146).

At the beginning, I introduced *mousikē,* a Greek art form where they danced, played music and recited poetry at the same time. The very word 'rhythm' emanates from this situation, which denotes a dancing body that moves in time as well as space. The dancer has no other purpose than the dance itself. One moves in dance, but despite this one stays in the same room. This is equivalent to the balance schema, a beautiful pattern standing still. The walker, however, moves towards a goal and has a direction. Walking might be fundamental to any motion.

Dance may be regarded as the mother of all arts because it uses time and space equally (Andrews 2017: 71–86). It still keeps the original situation of Greek *mousikē,* when temporal and spatial rhythm were used equally. With time, different genres developed, using rhythm in time – music, poetry – or rhythm in space such as pictures. Sculptures and houses may be apprehended as bodies in motion, where form details lead the regard in various directions (Hopsch 2008: ch. 4). Temporal art forms like music and poetry also move in a forward drive (Starr 2013: 87; Kühl 2003: 59; Olsson 1993). The phrase relates to the stanza and the entire poem, like the small motion of an arm relates to the body and to the surrounding landscape. A walk might be sequential in delightful patterns of stamp and trip or dynamic jumps. It would be possible to walk the most exquisite free verse if needed.

Dancing and walking demonstrate the two perception schemas investigated here, BALANCE and DIRECTION. Walking aims to reach a goal, even if one lingers in the beautiful scenery. If dance could be understood as a (lovely) condition, then walking relates to the moment of arrival. Whether one walks promptly or slowly, sooner or later one will arrive.

## Biorhythms

Understanding poetic rhythm as an outflow of biorhythms has consequences for interpretation. This could be seen in the four-step interpretation model of Chapter 3: the verse line (1) moves in some way, rising or falling, jumping or balancing; the movement might be (2) characterized; some kind of (3) emotion might be outlined; and then the signification is specified with the help of (4) the semantic context (p. 47).

The moving body can be regarded as a prototype for our discussion of aesthetic rhythm, as it continuously stages the interplay between the experiences of movement and balance. In this chapter, I have demonstrated that aesthetic rhythms may emanate from biorhythms such as walking, dancing, pulse, sex and breathing. Merleau-Ponty reflects that a body is both a physical structure and a lived experience, thereby representing two aspects of the bodily reality that are in play (Merleau-Ponty [1945] 2002; Varela, Thompson, and Rosch 1993: xv).

# 9

# Patterns of culture

## Convention

This chapter concentrates on the relationship between conventional and cognitive forms, or between traditional metres and free verse. The experience of rhythm is decided by a tension between cognitive factors and cultural conventions. The former ones consist of experiences like balance, direction, force and movement. The cultural elements are historically developed verse patterns. Meaning production uses both these possibilities. In Chapter 3, I pointed out that traditional forms during the centuries have accumulated certain signification – like the heroic qualities of the hexameter – and Chapter 8 concentrated on biorhythms as meaning producers.

In the seventeenth century, learned people constructed a system for the forms of emotion – a doctrine of affects (Nässén 2000). For example, young people were trained to associate an 'm' with death, because the Latin word for it is 'mors'. Today a stressed 'm' rather makes us think of chocolate, at least in Sweden, where a famous commercial used 'mmm' for a tasty delight. During the Baroque period, however, the association with 'm' was part of a training in rhetoric, as well as in the flourishing art of theatre.

Forms in this Baroque doctrine signify only according to convention, even if the founding fathers of rhetoric probably looked for some real similarity between form and world. Quintilianus, for example, ascribed decisive characters to certain figures. Long syllables create dignity, he says, and what is sublime needs sonority, and so on (Quintilianus 1922: 559). In time, these same connections between form and significance entered the reading mind and, even today, it is possible to grasp them because one was somehow trained that way. However, today, this training takes place subconsciously.

The metres developed slowly during the Renaissance. Many beautiful measures were created in Italy and southern France: sonnet, villanelle, rondeau and others. Mostly, they used the hendekasillaba – eleven syllables – as their line pattern. In time, these syllabic forms met with our verse system, the four-beat line of northern Europe, and an assimilation process took place. The strong stresses up north were adjusted to the limited number of syllables in the south, and gestalt pressure achieved Germanic iambs (Wagenknecht 1971). From the Renaissance, accent-syllabic metres became the dominant verse system in Germanic countries for some centuries.

## In the beginning was *Beowulf*

The Anglo-Saxon poem *Beowulf* has existed in handwritten form from about the year AD 1000, but was probably authored some centuries before that. The metrical form comes close to Old Norse versification. The most important rule concerns rhyming by alliteration. The stress was placed on the first syllable of a word, and this initial syllable is twice a line alliterated and thus emphasized. In *Beowulf*'s beginning lines below, alliteration is used to keep a long line together. This is oral poetry, and the reciter needed sound repetitions to remember the text (Ong [1982] 2002).

| Hwæt, we Gar-Dena / in geardagum, | oo OO o / o OO o |
| þeodcyninga / þrym gefrunon, | OO oo / O o O o |
| hu ða æþelingas / ellen fremedon! | oo O o O o / O o O oo |
| ... | (The beginning of *Beowulf*) |

[Listen! We have heard about the greatness of the people's kings of the Spear-Danes in old days, how nobility committed feat.][1]

As to versification rule, the line should have four prominences and be divided by a caesura in 2 + 2 stresses. Often these old texts are printed in short lines of two stresses each, which are kept together with the help of alliteration. The number of syllables in a long line varies between 8 and 16, but 10 to 11 syllables make up the most common length. Two ordinary speech phrases make one intonation phrase. The spondee OO is rather common, as can be seen in the notation above, where it appears twice in the first line and once in the second (Cable 1974: 360). The spondee functions badly together with tactus, but the rule of alternation had not yet been invented.

---

[1] I would like to thank Nils-Lennart Johannesson, Stockholm University, for reading, notation and translation.

The sequential accentual rhythm dominated in England up to ca. 1100 (Attridge 2012: 3). Together with the development of the new English language, a new tactus evolved with the imported limited space of the French verse line; there are two phases of the four-beat line, an older one that is sequential, and a younger one that is serial. Old Norse poetry develops different delicate measures out of the oldest uneven form, but if this happens in England nothing is left. After ca. 1100, the four beats become more evenly organized into what has been called stress-timed metre. In Germany, the *Niebelungenlied* (ca. 1200) demonstrates a half-developed metre. Here is a short excerpt in the Old Norse sequential measure *ljóðahattr*:

...

| ek veit einn | O o O | I know one thing |
| at aldri deyr: | o O o O | that never will die: |
| dómr of dauðan hvern. | O o O o O | the judgement on the deceased |
| | | (from 'Havamal') |

In the process of elaborating tactus, music had a decisive role. In the age of *Beowulf*, poetry happened in an oral performance with recitation and music together. The cadenced music may have influenced the recitation into tactus and, in time, such performances helped the gestalt pressure to create alternation (Creed 1990). The music used tactus, and French syllabism fortified a certain number of syllables (eight, for example), which, in the beginning, was very strange for Germanic literature. In time, these two influences together resulted in alternation – French syllabism and the music that accompanied oral performances (Wagenknecht 1971: 40, 72–3).

German poetry was the first linguistic region to adapt to the new pattern of tactus. There are traces in Otfried from the ninth century, but fully developed tactus first appeared in the thirteenth century (Gasparov 1996: 168). As for England, the change in rhythmic feeling followed the development of the new English language that took place after the Norman conquest, which is something that really brought French syllabism directly into the culture. Chaucer invented iambic metre (fourteenth century) and, after a break, it returned in the mid-sixteenth century (Attridge 2012: 5). Concerning Scandinavia, the new rhythmic design from continental Europe was accepted as late as the middle of the seventeenth century.

The medieval four-beat line of northern Europe continues the same outset – a verse schema that dominated for centuries. Different cultures moved on from this so-called doggerel verse at various times and, slowly, some kind of tactus was developed. The four-beat line allows the reciter to find the four stresses himself, which is why a normally weak syllable may suddenly become a beat, and a stress could be suppressed to keep four beats to a line (Attridge 2012: 6).

## The domination of tactus

The period of accent-syllabic versification lasted until approximately the beginning of the twentieth century. This era of serial rhythm produced many great measures – that is, rules for poetic form – meaning poems suddenly require an apparatus of scholarly knowledge.[2] The very old verse systems as well as modern ones – that both use sequential rhythm – are closer to spoken languages, as could be seen in *Beowulf*.

In spite of all the rules, tactus comes close to the body and seems rather primitive compared with, for example, Sappho's exquisite rhythms. During the historical period of tactus something happened to the readers; they developed a stern inner feeling for tactus, a gestalt pattern. Once this occurred, clever verse makers could work most daringly. Compare the severity of the eighteenth century with the soft metres of the nineteenth century. At the end of the nineteenth century, the reader would somehow save the tactus with the help of the flexibility of language, their own knowledge and an inner desire for the smoothness of heart beats. When modern poets at last left the tactus, they had to fight against this gestalt constraint. They certainly fought the versification rules, but these were easier to overcome than the gestalt pressure. Just look in the modernist manifestos!

However, different languages have reacted rather differently when handling the tactus. The German language, with its pointed stresses, makes tactus harder than the English language, which always seems to be on its way to lengthening syllables rather than simply stressing them. English tactus works in a smoother way compared with other Germanic languages.

A double iamb oO oO and a rising ionic oo OO are both similar and different. They both use four syllables and two stresses, and both are directed forward. However, iambs are serial and cadenced, but the ionic is sequential. The double

---

[2] I introduced the three principles of rhythm in Chapter 1, p. 17. Serial rhythm: tactus or beat in measured music and poetry. Sequential rhythm: the pattern of a phrase. Dynamic rhythm: the intensification towards a focus.

iamb spreads weaks and stresses evenly, but the ionic dramatizes the course and emphasizes the feeling when breaking with cognitive economy. However, iambs are more comfortable as well as economical (according to cognitive economy).

Conventions seem to prefer what is cognitively comfortable (Tsur 2017). Chapter 7 showed that tactus is economical in the sense that it, to a lesser extent, burdens the cognitive apparatus; the double iamb is handled more smoothly than the rising ionic. Or, the other way round, the conditions of the body are imperative for what is possible to do with poetic rhythm. In a second step, culture goes on embroidering; that is, shaping variations in accordance with the possibilities of the body.

## The sonnet: Ancient and modern

Old verse forms come close to speech rhythms, but with time rules of all kinds form aesthetic conventions. However, the modern free verse shows that conventions must be broken to regain expressivity. Tradition and free verse are playing with each other in a sonnet by Paul Muldoon. The sonnet is known precisely to be the metre that is most strained by heavy rules – even if the *sestina*, for example, is perhaps even more regulated. Anyhow, the sonnet is one of few classical measures that is still in use. Modern sonnet writers develop the old form in many ways; Muldoon combines regular rhymes with sequential rhythms and varied line lengths.

The origin of the sonnet is the Sicilian *strambotto* founded around AD 1230. The Italian version grew to be most popular – often named the 'Petrarcha sonnet' after Petrarcha's collection *Canzoniere* (1374). Shakespeare invented the English version. Muldoon plays with the Petrarchan form. A Petrarchan sonnet consists of fourteen lines in four parts. The first octet of eight lines in two stanzas are rhymed ABBA ABBA; that is, all rhymes are female (in two syllables) and more than two rhyme bands, A and B, are not allowed. The following six lines in two terzets also have female rhymes, but can vary from the preferred CDE CDE. In the languages of northern Europe, rhyming often uses only one syllable.

However, even more important than rhyming is the relationship between the octet and the following sextet. Something must happen between the first and the last half of the poem. The introducing eight lines shall present a subject, while the last six lines establish a new point of view. This change is called a *volta*, or turn.

Concerning line schemas, the sonnet has used various forms. French sonnets preferred the alexandrine,[3] while those in English were based in the iambic pentameter. With time, most cultures turned to the iambic pentameter as a base for the sonnet. But the four-beat line was also used as line schema in sonnets.

A Petrarchan sonnet makes the reader think of love – tradition has produced this meaning, and the love poem is one of the sonnet genres. Another one is the philosophical poem – the form of a sonnet agrees with intellectual reasoning. Fourteen lines of average length make a roomy space for thinking, and the *volta* offers a possibility to take a new perspective on the subject in question.

In spite of all its tricky rules, the sonnet has survived into modern poetry. Modern sonnets, however, like to break some of the rules – but not all of them. The format of 14 lines turned out to be vital. The classical printed picture of 4 + 4 + 3 + 3 lines has surely worked as a signal – here comes a sonnet – and during the last century it was certainly manipulated but is, broadly, still in use (Otterloo 1982; Lauvstad 1993). Many times the 14 lines are the only sonnet device, but Muldoon also makes use of the rhyme pattern and the *volta*.

A metre, like the sonnet, which is heavy with tradition and erudition, today brings weight as well as distance to its poem when pointing at the scholarly versification history. The modernist manifestos plead for a form as close as possible to meaning and significance, but the sonnet incarnates the very opposite with all its ornaments – perhaps it is more postmodern than modernist.

## Muldoon's sonnet

Muldoon's sonnet is a good example of a modern use of some versification rules, omitting others. This poem follows the sonnet rules according to the number of lines and the stanza composition. Rhymes are handled a little freely – aBaB cDcD efg efg – but keep to the genre. There is a *volta*, but it arrives one line too early, line 8 instead of line 9 as the rule prescribes. However, line schema and line lengths evidently break the versification rules. Here is 'More Geese':

    Now the sweep of the wing of a goose that had broken a child's arm
2  with a flying tackle
    on the next-but-one-farm
4  was cut short as the Romans had planned to cut the cackle

---

[3] oooooO / oooooO or, in Germanic languages, oOoOoO / oOoOoO.

of the geese on the Capitoline Hill
6 and utilised by the slattern
turned spick-and-span housewife to dust her sill.
8 They must be sacred still to some deity, these geese in a holding pattern

over the same pharmaceutical company's front lawn
10 on which their ancestors were staked
till their calls,

12 we hear, had drawn
down more geese flying north, must ache still as their ancestors ached
14 for the chance to fend off a night attack by the Gauls.

(Paul Muldoon, 'More Geese', *Maggot*, 2010)

There are two scenes from two different eras both taking place on the Capitoline Hill in Rome. The first one (l. 1–7) happens in the Roman Empire alluding to a historical episode from the year 387 BC. During a war with the Gauls, the holy geese of Juno's temple at the Capitoline Hill cackled vividly, warning the Roman soldiers, saving them from a nightly descent. So says Livius, whose story is well-known even today (*Ab Urbe Condita* book 5, ch. 47). The second scene (l. 8–14) belongs to our time. We are still in Rome and the Capitoline Hill, but now on the lawn of a modern pharmaceutical company. The geese, still flying north over the hill, are assumed to be longing for heroic achievements.

Grammar accompanies the time structure of the two scenes. Here there are only two sentences and only two grammatical subjects, 'the sweep (of the wing of a goose)' in the first line, and 'They' in line 8 alluding to 'these geese' of the same line. The change of subject initiates the *volta*. In spite of this grammatical severity there is room for more. In the first two stanzas, a goose wing hypothetically breaks the arm of a farmer's child, the Romans slaughter the geese, and a Roman housewife sweeps her house with a feather broom. After the *volta*, the reader meets with reflections over geese and their space in myth and history.

I think that Muldoon is kidding with Livius' story and its old-fashioned ideals of honour. The poem deviates from Livius' version in two cases – in the older text, the geese are honoured by the Romans, not killed, and the geese themselves are warning for the Gauls, independent of other geese that are 'flying north' (l. 13). The very title of the poem, 'More Geese', alludes to these extra birds. Muldoon seems to insinuate that the ancient geese were not able to save the Romans by themselves. Muldoon doubts Livius' heroic version, and points at the possible fate of Roman geese – they were probably slaughtered to make the feathered brooms – and, furthermore, Juno's geese would need help to be able to awaken the Roman army that night in the year 387 BC. But, of course, even the geese were proud Romans who were aching for heroic achievements. The two passages where Muldoon leaves Livius' story work as irony markers in the poem.

|    |                                  | Stresses | Rhymes | SSR          |
|----|----------------------------------|----------|--------|--------------|
| 1  | O o O oo O oo O / oo O oo OO     | 7        | a      | 2.3          |
| 2  | oo O o O o                       | 2        | B      | 3            |
| 3  | oo O o OO                        | 3        | a      | 2            |
| 4  | o OO / oo O oo O o O o O o       | 6        | B      | 2.3          |
|    |                                  |          |        |              |
| 5  | oo O oo O oo OO                  | 4        | c      | 2.5          |
| 6  | o O o 0 oo O o                   | 3        | D      | 2.7          |
| 7  | OO o OOO o O o O                 | 7        | c      | 1.4          |
| 8  | o O o O o O oo O oo / OO oo O o O o | 8     | D      | 2.5 (2.8–2)  |
|    |                                  |          |        |              |
| 9  | ooo O oo O oo O oo OO            | 5        | e      | 2.6          |
| 10 | o O o O ooo O                    | 3        | f      | 2.7          |
| 11 | oo O                             | 1        | g      | 3            |
|    |                                  |          |        |              |
| 12 | o O / o O>                       | 2        | e      | 2            |
| 13 | OOOO o O / o OO oo O oo O        | 9        | f      | 1.8 (1.2–2.5)|
| 14 | oo O oo O / o O o O oo O         | 5        | g      | 2.6          |

This is a sonnet because of its 14 lines grouped in the familiar four stanzas. The form of this poem mixes heavy tradition with a rhythm that comes close to ordinary speech. Rhymes occur according to the schema, while the 14 lines build a familiar pattern. However, the line lengths differ between one and nine stresses. Mostly, the rhythm goes forward; it is rising and alternates between zero and three weaks between stresses. This will hardly allow any feeling of tact; however, any text could be cadenced if one really tries.

Line lengths can be estimated by the number of stresses or number of syllables. In this poem, lengths vary between one stress or three syllables (l. 11) and nine stresses (l. 13) or nineteen syllables (l. 8). Deviant long lines are at least lines 1, 4, 8 and 13; that is, long lines arrive at certain distances in the text. There are some contrasts – the short lines 10 to 12 are surrounded by the long line 9 (five stresses, fourteen syllables) and line 13 (nine stresses and fifteen syllables).

Rhymes are inherently clean and, according to the rule, they are situated in line endings but, because of the varied line lengths, they arrive with irregular spacing. The long-liners 1 and 8 both prelude its half-poem, the octet (l. 1) and what happens after the *volta* (l. 8). As already said, the *volta* here arrives one line too early at line 8 instead of line 9 (as prescribed by the sonnet rule). The change of grammatical subject initiates the *volta*. Line 1 and line 8 both produce a kind of catapult effect.[4]

The stresses are situated most unevenly. Spondees OO vary with tribrachs ooo. Of the nine stresses in line 13, four construct a double spondee in the very beginning:

l. 13   down more geese flying north, must ache still as their ancestors ached
        OOOO o O                  o OO oo O oo O

9 stresses    (in half lines 5–4 stresses)
15 syllables  (in half lines 6–9 syllables)
Syllable stress ratio 1.8 (in half lines ratio 1.2–2.5)

Line 13 is pointed out as the kern of the poem 'More Geese'. The first half line presents an extreme rhythm. Of six syllables five are prominent. Furthermore, the beginning of line 13 continues an enjambment, which is why the last stress of line 12 might be added, 'drawn' O > OOOO o O.[5]

In line 13 the syllable stress ratio of the second half line is quite normal and comes close to common speech. The first half line, however, makes an extraordinary SSR of only 1.2; that is, most of it consists of prominences. The rising bacchius oOO 'must ache still' of the second half line echoes, once more, the emphasis of the preceding expression, 'had drawn/down more geese flying north' o O/OOOO o O. A low syllable stress ratio adds more to a long-liner than to a short line – the text becomes immensely heavy and distinguished as important. Otherwise, syllable stress ratios in this poem come close to normal speech.

The rhythm in this poem mostly goes forward – it is rising and mixed with zero to three weaks between stresses. This will hardly fortify any feeling of tactus. The writer seems to disturb any possibility of cadencing the poem. There

---

[4]  Line 8:1 could be read in various ways:
    ooo O o O oo O oo / but also:
    oO oOo O oOOoo / or: oO oO oO ooOoo / or: oO oO oO oO Ooo / or: oooOoOoOOoo /.

[5]  Stress clusters like this one are possible thanks to the various means of producing stress – pitch, length and pressure.

are many anapaests, but they are not allowed to take over. Line 1 would admit a reading with mixed tactus up to the very last words with a spondee stopping any cadence. The same manoeuvre repeats itself in line 3 and line 9. Line 6 runs rather evenly but ends up in the heavy jerking line 7. The same case repeats itself with the even lines 10 to 12, which land in the already discussed marked heaviness of line 13. These examples all show the poet fighting the traditional sonnet rhythm.[6]

So, the sonnet rule is violated in at least two aspects: line length and line schema. A vivid speech rhythm adds life and modernity to the traditional verse form that nonetheless is easily recognizable with its 14 lines in four traditional stanzas. The *volta* has also been played with when it arrives one line too early and divides the text in two equal parts – this way, losing the traditional charming irregularity of 8 + 6 lines. The placement of the *volta* focuses on line 8, which here opens up something new instead of closing the octet.

Muldoon seems to play jokes with Livius. In relation to Cohen, I discussed rhythm and irony (Chapter 6). As said, 'irony' is defined as two layers of meaning that fight each other. Irony markers tell the reader that something in the saying is inadequate, and the reader must try for some other signification. Irony markers in this poem are the two places where Muldoon's narrative does not agree with Livius' historical version, which will emerge as the subtext here. I would say that an average poetry reader still has some kind of knowledge about the mythical Capitoline Hill geese – they are now part of popular culture. With a raw laughter, the author pinpoints the possible fate of these geese – their wings were probably used for brooms. But the second layer, the subtext, reminds the reader of the heroic rumours about these geese.

The second occasion happens in line 13. I have already noted that the rhythmic heaviness of the first half line agrees with the title of the poem and points out line 13 as the main point of this poem. In this line, more geese than Juno's holy ones would be needed to save the Romans that night of 387 BC. Here Muldoon leaves Livius' narrative and insinuates that heroic achievements are mostly founded in wishful thinking rather than on historical correctness. The poem's attitude towards the geese is tender and spiteful at the same time.

The sonnet form connects this poem to the historical theme – it is old fashioned – even if Roman history and sonnet form belong to different eras. The connection rather points to the long tradition of respect to the ancient world,

---

[6] Compare with the interpretation model in Chapter 3, p. 47. Rhythmic devices create movements with their own characteristics and affects.

starting with the Renaissance. The severe verse form adds distance for readers who are used to modern free verse. At the same time, the jerking speech rhythm brings closeness, and the various spacing between rhymes – due to line length – plays down the historical serenity.

## Rules and expressivity

I started this chapter by saying that the experience of poetic rhythm exists in a tension between biorhythms and historically developed cultural patterns. Free verse has also developed patterns of its own. Muldoon's sonnet showed us how playing with tradition can be performed. Any other example will demonstrate this interaction in its own way. However, some conclusions are possible if one looks at history.

Above I cited the beginning lines from *Beowulf*. This old measure comes close to speech rhythm – ordinary speech has been stylized in a simple pattern of 2 + 2 stresses.[7] However, phrases are more salient here than in common speech; that which is well grouped will be easier to grasp as can be seen in Chapter 7. According to biorhythms, breathing needs intonation phrases of, perhaps, four stresses (Chapter 8). As it is well grounded in cognitive factors, such a form will be extremely lasting.

However, looking back at versification history, these old, rather simple forms carried into European culture, became stylized and equipped with rules.[8] Old Norse poetry, for example, developed plenty of metres through time. While advanced schemas for rhythm, rhymes and metaphors grew, they became more and more difficult to handle. Without scholarly knowledge writing poetry was quite impossible. The cultural tradition of tactus developed in a similar way. Verse forms aimed at increasing sophistication also accord cultural reputation as well as social status to the poet.

Such a development has its limits. Conventional forms create distance. Around the year 1900, poets started to break the rules in order to gain in expressivity. The delicate serial forms seemed to hold back the meaning of the poem and a new verse system broke through – free verse. The young modernists aimed at

---

[7] The four-beat line changes over time. The older forms emanate out of speech rhythm, but in time, during the influence of music, the form develops seriality. Attridge names this later variety 'dolnik' (Attridge 2012). Compare above page 133!

[8] Tsur notices as well that cultural products often are basically cognitive (2017: 19, fn 9).

underscoring signification with new technical means. Their ambitions can be studied in their many manifestos. They developed new cognitively expressive patterns with other kinds of strength. Many of the underlying patterns in old types of free verse were historically inspired (see p. 7); Old Norse and antique patterns govern their speech rhythms as well as Bible versification. In time, free verse also developed its own conventions.

In summary, in the history of versification, cognitive patterns, like these inspired of biorhythms, are primary. However, in a second step, cognitive forms tend to develop aesthetic conventions that add rules of all kinds. In a third step, conventions will be broken in order to regain expressivity to again favour cognitive possibilities. The development seems to happen like this:

- Cognitive patterns are primary.
- The cognitive form will be ascribed rules and conventions take over.
- Rules are broken to favour signification.

# 10

# Direction

## The promenade

There are many cognitive metaphors that thematize the path: 'Life is a path', 'Love is a path' and so on. The path, a course, implies direction in time and in space. Poets often say that they walk a poem – s/he needs to take a walk to get started. Walking seems to be the most important bodily rhythm when it comes to poetry. When walking, you leave one state of balance and head to a new point of balance. In between, your body, for a moment, is in a state of imbalance (Johnson 1987: 85–8). Balance works as a tense standing still. In promenading there is a kind of model for aesthetic rhythm.

The image schema of FORCE describes walks along a path (Johnson 1987: 45–7; Talmy 2000). This is important when looking at the two different cognitive metaphors of the future (Lakoff and Johnson 1999: 141–3). The first apprehends future events as passing you where you are – standing on the path of life. Music seems to be such an experience (Johnson 2007: 246–54). Music arrives at the listener only to disappear into the sea of time. The other metaphor pictures oneself walking along that path. Reading might be experienced as a walk through a book or a poem. The reader seems to be more in control.

However, a rhythmic course has a start and a goal, and a path that leads between them. One knows when one has reached the goal and the gestalt is closed. In between there are focus points and transport hauls. This forward movement is a kind of basic structure for the reading process, including its rhythmic course.

## Compulsion and diversion

This chapter investigates directions in poetic rhythm. There is always a forward drive (see Chapter 6). However, the forward movements are complicated in

> Music is said to have *narratives*. Ole Kühl, a jazz musician as well as a semiotician, has investigated directions in bebop music: its dynamic bows with beginning, focus and closure. The musical sequence moves towards focus, halts to rest and after that closes, and I presume that the phrase-rhythms of poetry behave in much the same way.
>
> Kühl means that rhythmic movement creates a kind of story, leaving something and arriving at something where one is able to stop and rest. The bebop story alternates between striving forward and a destination of rest. The telling consists in how to move towards the closure – it might meet more or less resistance, more or fewer detours (Kühl 2003: 58–65).
>
> The narrative is a basic structure of comprehension that even captures pieces of music. Kühl's idol is Miles Davis whose nickname used to be 'story teller'. An ordinary fairy tale, like *Little Red Riding Hood*, moves from moment to moment, with each one explaining the other. Grandma is eaten up *because* of the hunger of the wolf and so on. Peter Gärdenfors, the cognitive philosopher, points to a human need for causes, a compulsion for reasons, with evolutionary origins. If there is no reason, one will make one up (Gärdenfors 2006: 114–17).
>
> The time lapse of rhythm conducts us forward to fulfilment, and the walk is moving to-and-fro, the path passes peaks of intensity and instants of rest. The phrases of bebop linger at its destination after bunches of detours that develop the tension. Listening to this could be just as exciting as wolf hunting.

various ways; they are met with counterforces as well as pushed by devices like enjambment and flow.

We have already met with a Sexton poem (Chapter 2). Another one, a love poem from 1969, can show how directions work in a poem. This poem pictures a daring scene of love making that is described with bold metaphors and centres on the sensations of the (two) folds of the knee. The two persons here are the 'I' (l. 7) and 'my darling' (l. 4). From the perspective of rhythm, telling goes swiftly and lightly, especially in the beginning, but here is also an anomaly in line 10 – a whole line of only stresses. The many enjambments underline a strong forward movement.

|   |   |   |
|---|---|---|
|   | Being kissed on the back | ooO ooO > |
| 2 | of the knee is a moth | ooO ooO > |
|   | at the windowscreen and | ooOoo0 0 > |
| 4 | yes my darling a dot | O oOo oO > |
|   | on the fathometer is | oooOoo 0> |
| 6 | tinkerbelle with her cough | Ooo ooO |

|    |                              |                |
|----|------------------------------|----------------|
|    | and twice I will give up my  | oO oooO 0 >    |
| 8  | honor and stars will stick   | Oo oO oO       |
|    | like tacks in the night      | oO ooO         |
| 10 | yes oh yes yes yes two       | O O OOO O>     |
|    | little snails at the back    | ooO ooO >      |
| 12 | of the knee building bon-    | ooO OoO >      |
|    | fires something like eye-    | Oo Ooo O>      |
| 14 | lashes something two zippos  | Oo Oo OOo      |
|    | striking yes yes yes small   | Oo OOO O       |
| 16 | and me maker.                | o OO o         |

(Anne Sexton, 'Knee Song', *Love Poems*, 1969)

The promenade is a sub-pattern to the dominating perceptual pattern of FORCE. Characteristics for the image schema of FORCE are intensity and directionality (Johnson 1987: 43–4). It is possible to transfer these devices to the circumstances of versification; intensity concerns heaviness – much of length, amplitude and pitch. Line 10 in Sexton's poem with six stresses together is characterized by an extreme intensity as well as by heaviness.

The basic form of FORCE makes a natural forward movement. But the motion might be disturbed. In the case of poetry, the line breaks will prevent the movement when reshaping the gestalts in new ways. The basic forward direction meets with counterforce. Mark Johnson differentiates several types of counterforces, and here I have chosen a couple of them that are easily recognizable in versification (Johnson 1987: 42–8, especially 45–7). Ordinary force structures that operate constantly in our experience – all common knowledge when taking a walk – are 'compulsion', 'blockage', 'counterforce', and 'diversion'. In the actual poem there is a strong compulsion forward in the very beginning:

|       |                              |             |
|-------|------------------------------|-------------|
|       | Being kissed on the back     | ooO ooO >   |
| l. 2  | of the knee is a moth        | ooO ooO >   |
|       | at the windowscreen and      | ooOoO 0 >   |
| l. 4  | yes my darling …             | O oOo …     |

The very quick anapaests open the poem with a forward movement that is even strengthened by many enjambments. Because of the forward rush, ordinary line break pauses are weaker than usual, and there is no real clash in the lapse of this poem – the blockage will not arrive before the end:

|       |               |         |
|-------|---------------|---------|
|       | …             |         |
| l. 16 | and me maker. | o OO o  |

This very last line changes style, the grammar cramps, rhythm balances and the reader is rapidly transferred from body to soul.

The two weaker kinds of diverging force, what Johnson calls 'counterforce' and 'diversion', make two degrees of ambiguity. In both these cases, there are two directions in play, where the basic forward movement is met with resistance or distraction. The line break makes a counterforce but in this poem they are special, as most of them involve enjambments that shrink the pause.

In addition, repetition disturbs the basic forward movement. The reader is forced to look back to the first occurrence, which makes the text in between the two cases ring in the reading mind. This kind of ambiguity may exemplify Johnson's 'diversion' as well as Tsur's back-structuring and Jakobson's equivalences. Repetitions in this poem are, for example, the returning sensitive back of the knees, the many times that 'yes' is repeated, the driving anapaests from the beginning that return in lines 11–12, and the repeated marked enjambments with their special pronunciation of slowing down and lengthening sounds. Line breaks (counterforces) and repetitions (diversions) are two significant distinguishing features of poetry.

## Rising and falling rhythm

Traditionally, versification studies have emphasized the difference between so-called rising and falling tactus. In metered versification, the directions are said to follow the first syllable of the line. If this is a stress, the direction falls; if it is a weak syllable, the direction rises. Also, free verse rises and falls on the basis of a focus that semantically distinguishes the most prominent point of a line or a phrase, causing the rising and falling movements. The weaker parts group around a strong kernel – this is the prolongation scheme with goal, anticipation and extension (Cureton 1992: 146–9). If focus occurs late in the phrase or line, there is a rising movement, and in the opposite case, there is a falling movement.[1] A phrase like o OO o 'and me maker' (l. 16) just rests (Talmy 2000: 414). Two pictures

---

[1] When discussing movements in the verse line, Reuven Tsur explores the perceptual forces of Rudolf Arnheim's visual diagrams (Arnheim 2004). He demonstrates how audible figures are perceived in the same way as visual ones. Motion in visual figures appears analogously in the acoustic gestalts of lines and phrases in poetry. When focus comes close to the gestalt border, perceptual forces create the impression of motion within patterns or gestalts. Intrusion in the middle of a unit gives balance and stability but asymmetric intrusion creates forces (Tsur 2011).

of Carmen show the movements of rising and falling, forward and backward. In Figure 10.2 below, she moves forward to the right (in the reading direction), while in Figure 10.1 she looks backwards. The rising, forward movement follows the time arrow, while the falling, backward look complicates time.

Rising and falling movements are most important for the rhythm of a poem. It is not indifferent if a line or a phrase starts with a strong or a weak syllable. Reuven Tsur has demonstrated what happens to the gestalts in these two cases (Tsur 2011, 2017: 210–29). A stress consists of three parts: length, pitch and amplitude. The prominence in a rising context (iambs, anapaests) uses in the first place length or extended time, while the one in a falling context uses amplitude. This means that the weak part of the rising iamb will be short and volatile, and the two weaks of an anapaest will be even more so. In comparison, the weak part of a trochee is rather tardy and stable – it tries to resist change. A sequence of iambs can easily adjust the relationship between pitch, length and amplitude, while the trochees like to show off their weak parts (Kruckenberg and Fant 1993).

The quick and volatile iambs create a rapid tempo for rising lapses, but the stable, falling trochees linger. As Tsur has shown, iambs contrast their strong and

**Figure 10.1** Looking backwards. In this picture, the centre of gravity lies to the left but Carmen's bottom and feet to the right also takes place. 2012. Photo © Nobu Yamamoto.

**Figure 10.2** Carmen takes a stride in a forward falling movement, almost at the limit of losing control. The French word 'enjambment' could be translated 'to stride'. 2012. Photo © Nobu Yamamoto.

weak parts; when parts of an iamb, the strong one grows even longer and the short one shrinks. Trochees, however, want to even out the text; the strong, stressed syllable is not so strong, and the weak part expands. In emotive passages, the weak part of a trochee is strengthened while the iamb underlines its prominence. Iambs make intensity with the help of speed and energy, but trochees create it through repeated weight. Readers prefer rising rhythms, says Tsur. Falling figures are kind of unnatural because of their heavy beginnings (Tsur 2017: 24, 26, 40, 50).

Sexton's poem mingles the rising and falling lines, in this way, to shape the feeling:

|  |  |  |
|---|---|---|
|  | … |  |
|  | on the fathometer is | oooOoo 0> |
| l. 6 | tinkerbelle with her cough | Ooo ooO |
|  | and twice I will give up my | oO oooO 0 > |
| l. 8 | honor and stars will stick | Oo oO oO |
|  | … |  |

In this passage, every other line passes very quickly (l. 5, 7), and every other one underlines its saying (l. 6, 8). The 'fathometer' of line 5 rushes by only to underline what happens around the line break, 'is tinkerbelle' OOoo. The same device takes place in line 7, which determinedly is directed to 'give up my honor' 0O OOo. The lingering reading of the enjambments goes together with preluding stresses of line 6 and line 8, thus creating slow and heavy points in the flow.

A rising direction is in accordance with ordinary bodily movements. A person normally walks forward. Talking about temporality, a rising movement is consistent with time that also moves forward (cf. Chapter 6). From this perspective, rising rhythms are unmarked, while falling rhythms are marked. The uncomplicated forward motion, from the light parts to the heavy parts, goes with scientific time that moves invariably forward.[2] Falling motion works as a diversion.

I have mentioned several times already the anapaests that dominate the flow of this poem. There are two passages that only consist of anapaests, lines 1–3 and lines 11–12, in addition to the many occasional occurrences. In this love-making process they add a quality of smoothness – of no resistance.

|  |  |  |
|---|---|---|
|  | Being kissed on the back | ooO ooO > |
| l. 2 | of the knee is a moth | ooO ooO > |
|  | at the windowscreen and | ooO ooO > |
|  | … |  |

---

[2] Also compare with semiotic phenomena like 'deixis' and 'index' (Brandt and Cronquist 2019).

|  | little snails at the back | ooO ooO > |
|---|---|---|
| l. 12 | of the knee building bon- | ooO ooO > |
|  | fires something like eye- | Oo Ooo O> |
| l. 14 | lashes something two zippos | Oo Oo OOo |

...

In lines 1–3, the weaks are a little more pregnant than in lines 11–14, even if this small difference does not appear in the notation. Here 'Being' (l. 1) might take a little more space, just like 'windowscreen' Oo0 in line 3. However, the tempo increases with the second passage lines 11–12 that rushes forward until 'bon-fires something' OOo Oo – a movement that is also repeated in the next line pair lines 13–14: 'eye-lashes something' OOo Oo. This love making hovers between easy running and loaded moments.

Falling rhythm, however, plays with two forces: the forwardness of the course and the backwardness of attention. Rising rhythm hurries forward to something, while the falling ones tardily move away from something. But, of course, one

---

*The Kalevala*

The old Finnish form of *rune metre* moves very slowly. The pattern consists of 4 + 4 trochees in line pairs, where the second half line repeats what is said in the first one. The rule prescribes alliteration but no end rhyming. All the trochees take their time and the repetitions take even more; at least one will feel so when reading the *Kalevala*, and measuring reading time will, for sure, confirm that impression.

| Kullervo, Kalervon poika, | Kullervo, son of Kalervo, |
|---|---|
| Sinisukka äijön lapsi, | Blue stocking, the child of the old man, |
| Siitä suorikse sotahan, | Prepares for fight, |
| Vainotielle valmistaikse. | Girts himself for war |

...

Nature offers two models for time: the forward time arrow and the spiral time of nature with its steady repetitions (Chapter 6). The rune metre uses them both, but the spiral pattern dominates. The spiral movement holds back the narrative in a repeated looking back – reading the *Kalevala* is like rowing against the headwind, a diversion. However, this national epic of Finland gives the patient reader an unforgettable experience.

must always move to the right, quickly or tardily, according to the time arrow and the reading direction.[3]

In this poem the lines 4, 6, 8, 10 and 13–15 are falling, especially in the very end, lines 13–15, where they move heavily. A falling figure makes time go slower, as could be seen when I discussed iambs contra trochees apropos lines 13–14, and in other passages. Falling motion works as a diversion – a kind of rowing against the headwind. Versification literature sometimes says that falling rhythmic movement goes backwards, but of course this is not possible. Here psychological time plays jokes with the reader. Some versification devices spatialize time, like repetitions.

## Enjambment

Many times in this book, I have observed all sorts of enjambments in the notations. The enjambment underlines the forward movement, at the same time as it complicates it. Enjambment is a common device in free verse, and the conflict between verbal phrase and lineation makes it a preferred method of pointing to the very condition of poetry, as it denotes the line break as its defining device (Kjørup 2003: 239–54; 2008). The line of about three seconds should be kept together, as the gestalt of the short-term memory basically decides any pattern in a poem. The stanza or the small phrase play around by relating to this basic pattern, and a pointed enjambment may be experienced as both salient and confusing (Tsur 2012a: 217).

Above I referred the forward movements in poems to the cognitive schema of FORCE and also pointed to various counterforces. The enjambment adds a complication. The movement of the line is fulfilled at the line break, but the movement of the phrase will continue. The chasm of the line break is defeated by the coherence of the phrase. The repeated line-break pause, about half a second long, will be filled by the peculiar extension of the last syllable that can be extended.

There are different grades of enjambments, weaker and stronger, depending on the closeness of grammatical proximity in the phrase. As the weak ones are less of a problem, I have only noted strong enjambments, where the parts of the divided phrase really stand close together, like 'give up my/honor' (l. 7) or 'the back/of the knee' (l. 11). But even in these cases, the handling of the enjambment

---

[3] I refer only to Germanic languages. Languages like Hebrew and Chinese have other reading directions.

depends on the reader.[4] It is possible to forget about the line break and just continue without changing pitches or lengths. One may also read the other way around, by making a stop in the line break, thereby leaving clause coherence to its fate. However, the writer meant something when construing this enjambment, and good interpretation should take care of line as well as of phrase.

In marking the line break, but still in contact with the phrase, coherence will create the special rhythm of a run-on line, which is the special slowing down and lengthening of sounds. The line-break pause usually lasts about half a second, but now it will be saturated with the extra weight on the last syllable that is possible to extend – if not the very last one, the preceding one or the next one in order (antepenultima). In Sexton's poem most end syllables are easily given extra length but some of them would be weak if found in another position, like 'and' (l. 3), 'is' (l. 5) and 'my' (l. 7).

So, the many enjambments cause a rhythmic distortion that produces significance and feelings:

...
l. 10    yes oh yes yes yes two           O O OOO O>
         little snails at the back        ooO ooO >
l. 12    of the knee ...                  ooO

The reading of the enjambments puts a heavy weight on 'two' and 'back'. After the exclamation in line 10, the following 'two' bridges the line-break gap with the help of its pronounced length. There are two folds of the knee, and it is the fold that is important here. Here the enjambments make a rush between the 'yes' and the 'bon-fires' of lines 12–13.

There is one more circumstance that shapes the unyielding forward movement. Every vowel peaks somewhere, and normally this happens in its very beginning.[5] However, with the special reading of an enjambment the peak comes late, often very late, in the vowel, which is something that creates the effect of (almost) falling or stumbling – of (almost) breaking the gestalt in its steep forward movement. The late peaking effect is about milliseconds, but one can still hear the deviation.

---

[4] Frank Kjørup has made a useful classification of enjambments out of reading choices (Kjørup 2008: 83–101).

[5] Here Tsur (2012a: 224) reports Gerry Knowles's findings concerning early and late peaking. Tsur and Knowles have investigated poetry readings made by established actors.

The most remarkable enjambments in the Sexton poem are the two compounded, but divided, words of lines 12–14. Here the verbal cohesion is stronger than in the other cases:

| l. 12 | … building bon- | OoO > |
| | fires something like eye- | Oo Ooo O> |
| l. 14 | lashes something … | Oo Oo |

I have pointed at the rhythmic rush towards the loaded moments of 'bonfires' OOo and the tickling 'eye-lashes' OOo. The words are cut in two pieces, that way loading the tension to a maximum in the end of this love-making scene.

As said above, the strong FORCE of this poem has no real blockages until the end. They burst forwards in a rush that is nuanced by the rising and falling movements. One should read it in one breath, one gestalt. This love making starts at high speed and slows down in the lines about the fathometer, and then speeds up again until the remarkable line 10, which consists of only stresses.

Of course, all these prominences of line 10 may be interpreted with slight variations. The 'oh' and the 'two' of the enjambment could be a little weaker, and all the 'yeses' may slightly vary in pitch and length. This line stands out in its heaviness, and here the love making approaches its culmination when returning to the folds of the knee. As the title says, this is a 'Knee Song'.

| | … | |
| l. 10 | yes oh yes yes yes two | O 0 OOO 0> |
| | little snails at the back | ooO ooO > |
| l. 12 | of the knee building bon- | ooO ooO > |
| | fires something like eye- | Oo 0ooO> |
| l. 14 | lashes something two zippos | Oo 0o OOo |
| | striking yes yes yes small | Oo OOO O |
| l. 16 | and me maker. | o OO o |

From line 10, the accelerated enjambments carry us over to a falling, emphasizing movement that runs out in the balanced, majestic end line. The emphasis of lines 11–14 leans on the funny constructions of the line endings of line 12 and line 13, where a word is cut in two pieces, that way loading the reader's attention and augmenting the tension. In line 15 the exclamation from line 10 returns once more before the balanced paramount end line.

## Flow

Rhythmic flow is another way to underline the basic forward direction in poems, here with the help of increasing the tempo. In the Introduction (p. 8), I distinguished between some types of free verse and also mentioned the Bible style that emanated out of Walt Whitman's experiments with Psaltar rhythms – when talking about the Psaltar I refer to translations, mainly those in the King James's Bible.[6] This free-verse tradition is characterized by a strong forward movement, long lines and repetitions. Cumulated weaks change with spondees. There is an American tradition of free verse in Bible style (Sandburg, Ginsburg), and in the 1910s it became à la mode in Europe. European surrealists often preferred this form (Breton). Its streaming character somehow could emphasize the streaming of the subconscious.

To a great degree, this kind of versification depends on the repeated intonation phrase that shapes a dominant bow from a low pitch to a high one, and then to a low (Arnholtz 1960). The small phrases disappear into the streaming sound flow. The amount of sound makes the reader hurry up. Within this frame, tempo may change with the intention of showing what is important. In versification terms, cumulated weaks alternate with spondees and molossi, and the reading tempo alternates between rapid strains and slower ones that aim at contrast.

'Flow' has been used as a psychological concept and is defined as an optimal experience of focused awareness. Action and consciousness are the same – one is concentrated and calm. There is a sense of control, ease and fun (Chemi 2016: 46). In this description, one may recognize what I here would like to call the Boccioni. I will add that the euphoric experience of totally concentrating involves a strong direction towards a focus. However, the deep concentration and calm also means a kind of balance. This cooperation between a strong forward movement and balance could be illustrated by the Hermes sculpture by the Italian futurist Umberto Boccioni (1882–1916) shown in Figure 10.3 below.

Boccioni was a painter and a sculptor. He even wrote the manifesto for the futurist painters. In his own art, he focused on the representation of speed, and his bronze sculptures roar from air-vents – a paradox, yes, a sculpture has to balance. Otherwise it would fall down.

---

[6] Emmilou Grosser has investigated the Hebrew long-liners of the Old Testament (Grosser 2017, 2023).

**Figure 10.3** Hermes on the run. Umberto Boccioni, 'Unique Forms of Continuity'. 1913. Metropolitan Museum of Art.

Boccioni's figures look like dashing forward, and the same impression could be found in some poetry, a streaming forwardness together with stability:

> I believe a leaf of grass is no less than the journey-work of the stars,
> And the pismire is equally perfect, and a grain of sand, and the egg of
>     the wren,
> ...
>
> (Walt Whitman, 'Song of Myself', 31, l. 1–2.<br>*Leaves of Grass*, 1855)

OoOoOoO / oOO / ooOoOooO
ooOOo oOooOo / ooOoO / ooOooO

# 11

# Balance in versification

## Balance in versification

DIRECTION is a strong image schema of special interest for aesthetic rhythm. A second one is that of BALANCE (Johnson 1987: 85). 'Balance' is a term in classical rhetoric where it points towards the figure of parallelism (Nordman 1987: 13). Basically, balance is part of an essential, spatial comprehension, starting from the vertical line of a standing body within the frame of a gestalt. In Chapter 4, I have demonstrated how this spatial perception also involves time-based forms (Murray 1995: 95–6; Johnson 2018: 252–5).

In my Introduction, I recalled the image of a tightrope walker to clarify how balance works in a piece of art (p. 10). A directed movement also needs balance – bodily and cognitively. Every step taken includes direction, losing control and a regained balance. As the tightrope walker shows, equilibrium is not something static – it is balance at work. A balancing figure somehow rests in the centre of a field of tension. Look at Boccioni's 'Bottle'! If a rising direction pushes on time and a falling direction makes it stagnant, balance works on holding it back. A perfect balance means a dynamic standing still, including a tendency to imbalance.[1]

I have pointed out several times that temporal courses are perceived as spatial gestalts. Time-based art forms like music and poetry work with proportions and relations between proportions just like spatial art forms. A good example of this spatialization is the back-structured figures that are investigated by Tsur (Tsur 2012a: 302–3). A gestalt must be closed before patterning, and one grasps the form backwards. The temporal course includes a spatial understanding that is caused by gestalt pressure.

---

[1] See also Chapter 8, pp. 109–11, where I compare walking with dancing. When walking, one is directed forward; when dancing one is staying in the room even if arms and legs shape occasional directions.

**Figure 11.1** Umberto Boccioni, 'Development of a Bottle in Space'. 1913. Compare with Boccioni's interpretation of Hermes dashing through the heavens in Figure 10.3. Metropolitan Museum of Art.

In Chapter 5 I investigated the FORCE schema in relation to Ferlinghetti's poem (p. 70). Among other things, I said that FORCE is connected to gravity and its bodily reactions. DIRECTION and BALANCE are both sub-schemas to FORCE (Johnson 1987). But FORCE also works in the material of language. Lines and phrases are acoustic entities. Bodily experience of balance includes weight and pressure (Johnson 1987: 85, 98). Verbal 'weight' may be understood as length and intensity or simply as more sound. Stresses are heavier than weak syllables. 'Pressure' forces direction into its goal (see Chapters 5 and 10). Take a look at Figure 11.2 below. The arrows point out how the forces work.

According to the line, one can measure the degree of heaviness with the help of the syllable stress ratio, where 1 means that all syllables in the line are prominent, 2 means that half of the number is prominent, and so on (Hrushovsky 1954: 244, 251). Semantic weight strengthens the acoustic weight.

## How to balance

The poem for us to follow in this chapter is borrowed from Ted Hughes' *Birthday Letters*, a book of about 80 poems, where the author at last tells us his own version of his marriage to Sylvia Plath. Here I will demonstrate how the image schema of BALANCE can be transferred into versification studies.

>     There you are, in all your innocence,
> 2   Sitting among your daffodils, as in a picture
>     Posed as for the title: 'Innocence'.
> 4   Perfect light in your face lights it up
>     Like a daffodil. Like any one of those daffodils
> 6   It was to be your only April on earth
>     Among your daffodils. In your arms,
> 8   Like a teddy bear, your new son,
>     Only a few weeks into his innocence.
> 10  Mother and infant, as in the Holy portrait.
>     And beside you, laughing up at you,
> 12  Your daughter, barely two. Like a daffodil
>     You turn your face down to her, saying something.
> 14  Your words were lost in the camera.
>                             And the knowledge
> 16  Inside the hill on which you are sitting,
>     A moated fort hill, bigger than your house,
> 18  Failed to reach the picture. While your next moment,
>     Coming towards you like an infantryman
> 20  Returning slowly out of no-man's-land,
>     Bowed under something, never reached you –
> 22  Simply melted into the perfect light.
>                 (Ted Hughes, 'Perfect Light', *Birthday Letters*, 1998)

This poem describes a photo of a young woman with her two small children. The speaker comments on it – especially the role of the blooming daffodils. He also compares it to the iconography of the Madonna. After line 15 the picture darkens. An arriving threat compares the idyll to a situation of war. The lovely daffodils hint at Wordsworth's famous poem and compares the young woman of this poem with his lonely wanderer.

The immediate impression of the poetic rhythm here is a high syllable stress ratio in the longer first part of the poem and a lower one after line 18, where the threat is introduced. A careless speech rhythm dominates the first part, while the second part uses a poetic language that is heavy with symbols.

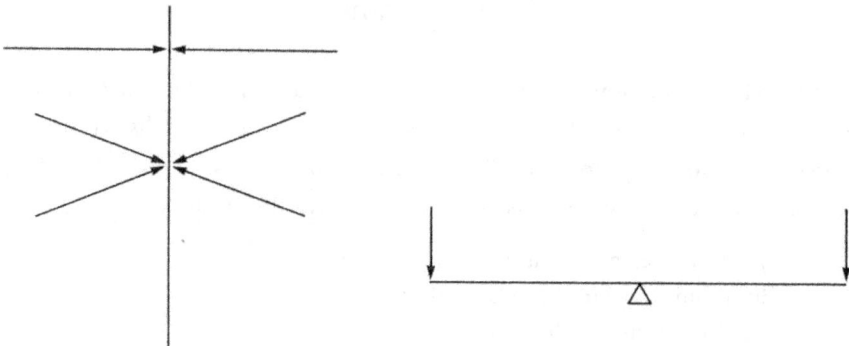

**Figure 11.2** Axis balance and twin pan balance. The arrows mark how forces influence the balance points. Mark Johnson, *The Body in the Mind,* 1987: 86. University of Chicago Press.

The BALANCE schema contains force, direction and weight. Mark Johnson points out how body image schemas of BALANCE can be interpreted as *axis balance* and *twin pan* balance (Johnson 1987: 85–6). Both these schemas are recognized through our own bodily experiences of balance and point out how balance can be understood as an activity. Take a look at Figure 11.2 above, which describes the axis balance and the twin pan balance. The arrows show how the forces work.

Axis balance and twin pan balance also involve the sound stream of a poem. Phrases may balance within themselves (axis) but also balance each other (twin pan). In the first case, there is an axis in the phrase – 'Your daughter' oOo – and in the second case there are two stress points – as is the case in the two succeeding phrases 'Like a daffodil' ooOoo (l. 12) and 'in the camera' ooOoo (l. 14).

- Form segments may be in internal balance (axis).
- Form segments may balance each other (twin pan).

In Chapter 6, I distinguished between four gestalt levels in a poem – the phrase, the line, the stanza and the whole poem. They seem to prefer their own ways to balance the sound stream:

- The small phrase and the line may use axis balance.
- Phrases and lines also may balance each other – twin pan balance.
- Stanzas and whole poems preferably work with twin pan balance.
- The printed picture of the whole poem may use axis balance.

Axis balance prefers small entities like the three small balanced phrases of line 12. Here, the axis is marked with boldface in the notation:

...
l. 12   Your daughter, barely two. Like a daffodil      oOo / OoO // ooOoo
...

However, turning to the visuality of a poem, axis balance may be a strong factor, which is something that could be seen in Chapter 5 where the Ferlinghetti poem contained an extra twist with the help of its somewhat unsteady printed picture (p. 70). The entire poem resembles a fat-bellied fellow swaying on his right foot in an attempt to achieve balance.

In free versification, twin pan figures are a hallmark. Form elements that are internally imbalanced balance each other in repeated acoustic sequences. A usual construction of rhythm in a free verse poem emanates from directed asymmetric sequences in motion, that are imbalanced within themselves but gallantly balance another asymmetric sequence, as could be seen in the repeated adonius Ooo Oo in the beginning of lines 16, 19 and 21 of Hughes' poem.

After that, the cretic OoO returns twice in line 4: The cretic of the title 'Perfect light' OoO (axis balance) is repeated (twin pan balance) in the very first phrase of Hughes' poem:

l. 1   There you are/ ...                          OoO /
l. 4   Perfect light in your face lights it up     OoO/ooO/OoO

In line 22 ('Perfect light' OoO), it closes the poem.

I would say that the four cretici of the title up to line 4 work cohesively, but the very last phrase of the poem, to a certain degree, does the same as it is helped by its position – the very last figure stands out – as well as the word repetition, 'perfect light', which returns here for the third time. There are also other repeated figures, like the spondees OO in two groups, first in lines 5, 8, 9 and in the other part of the poem in lines 17, 18 with a strengthened version in line 20 – the molossus 'no-man's-land' OOO.

Reading time moves forward of course, but the repetitions direct the attention backwards, and in that course the 'now' will expand. Time seems to stand still just like a body in balance, as in the neighbouring line endings in Hughes' poem:[2]

---

[2]   Johnson (1987: 85). The cognitive metaphor BALANCE IS EQUIVALENCE connects Jakobson's theory of equivalence (1960: 358) with a cognitive model.

| | | | Like a daffodil | ooOoo |
| l. (5,) 12 | ... | | | |
| | ... | | | |
| l. 14 | ... | | in the camera. | ooOoo |
| | ... | | | |

The connection of the two cadences creates a kind of stop effect in line 14, where the poem will change both in style and in atmosphere. Instead of rushing over to the short line 15, attention is directed backwards to the last daffodil of this poem in a beautiful twin pan balance.

With the rhythmic change that occurs below the middle of this poem (l. 17), the delight in the picture of the young mother and her two children is replaced with a threat of desolation, and the rhythm differs considerably between the two parts, as can be seen in the notation below. Before line 16, there are syllable stress ratios of up to 4, signalling speech language, but in the last part the stress ratios are lower.

| | | Line lengths | | Syllable stress ratio | |
|---|---|---|---|---|---|
| | | Stresses | Syllables | Line | Phrase |
| | OoO / oOoOoo | 4 | 9 | 2.25 | 1.5–3 |
| 2 | OooOoOoo / oooOo | 4 | 13 | 3.25 | 2.7–5 |
| | OoooOo / Ooo | 3 | 9 | 3 | 3–3 |
| 4 | OoO ooO OoO | 5 | 9 | 1.8 | 1.25–3–1.25 |
| | ooOoo // oOoO oOOoo | 5 | 14 | 2.8 | 5–2–2.25 |
| 6 | oOoO oOoOo oO | 5 | 11 | 2.2 | |
| | oOoOoo // ooO | 3 | 9 | 3 | 3–3 |
| 8 | ooOoOo / oOO | 4 | 9 | 2.25 | 3–1.5 |
| | OooOO oooOoo | 4 | 11 | 3.8 | 1.7–6 |
| 10 | OooOo / oooOoOo | 4 | 12 | 3 | 2.5–3.5 |
| | ooOo / OoOoo | 3 | 11 | 3.7 | 4–2.5 |
| 12 | oOo / OoO // ooOoo | 4 | 11 | 2.75 | 3–1.5–5 |
| | oOoO OoO / OoOo | 6 | 11 | 2.2 | 2.3–2 |
| 14 | oOoO ooOoo | 3 | 11 | 3.7 | 2–5 |
| | ooOo | 1 | 4 | 4 | |
| 16 | OooO oOooOo | 4 | 10 | 2.5 | 2–3 |
| | oOooOO / OoooO | 5 | 10 | 2 | 1.7–2.5 |
| 18 | OoOoOo // OoOOo | 6 | 11 | 1.8 | 2–1.7 |
| | OooOo ooOooO | 4 | 11 | 2.75 | 2.5–3 |
| 20 | oOoOo OoOOO | 6 | 10 | 1.7 | 2.5–1.25 |
| | OooOo / OoOo | 4 | 9 | 2.25 | 2.5–2 |
| 22 | OoOo oooOoO | 4 | 10 | 2.5 | 2–3 |

period //
comma /
new phrase – blank

**Figure 11.3** Axis balance, or approximately standing still. Forms in a perceived equivalence point at the bodily experience of walking. Carmen's axis is her own backbone. The salience of the irregularity of Carmen's bent knee makes the balance extra expressive. As said in Chapter 7 (pp. 97, 99), a small asymmetry creates better reader attention than complete similarity. 2012. Photo © Nobu Yamamoto.

In the table above, I have also registered the line lengths of the poem. Two measures could be used – the number of stresses and number of syllables. Here they are both quite normal. The number of syllables circles around the 10 to 11 ones that cooperate with tradition and short-term memory, and the number of phrases is mostly two as they should be within such a span. This is a normal line structure in a poem that exemplifies the Nordic type of free verse (see p. 7). It is not disturbed by any strong enjambments. However, some lines are determinedly divided by firm breaks (periods in l. 5, 7, 12, 18 and also many commas), which makes the small phrases distinct.

In the description of the photo (l. 1–14), the poem moves quickly from detail to detail. The swiftness relates to a high number of weaks – I have already pointed out that syllable stress ratios here are higher than usual. Line 2–3, and 9–10 are characterized by a returning tribrach ooo that is also repeated in lines 17 and 22. The tribrachs turn up in pairs, in two succeeding lines, in twin pan balances. Another returning figure is the spondee, and there is a twin pan balance in lines 8–9, where the baby is described with the help of a repeated spondee:

> ...        In your arms,
> l. 8 Like a teddy bear, your new son,         ooOoOo / oOO
> Only a few weeks into his innocence.    OooOO oooOoo         SSR 1,7–6
> ...

Line 9 contains a sharp contrast between the heavy first part and the extremely light second part, with syllable stress ratios of 1.7 and 6. And, in the same way, the first piece of the poem moves between very swift and more chiselled parts.

The flow of the initial description is broken by two word repetitions, 'daffodils' and 'innocence'. I will comment on the repeated 'daffodils' in the next section. The position of the repeated 'innocence' of lines 1, 3 and 9 is the last word of each line, giving it extra weight. These three uses of 'innocence' work like an end rhyme in twin pan balances.

The rhythm of lines 17–21 differs from the light-hearted first part of the poem. A terrible menace approaches the young woman, a threat that is prepared in line 6 already, when emphasizing the fragility of the daffodils. The rhythm is characterized by spondees OO, adonii OooOo, and low stress ratios. There are no tribrachs ooo here where the creepy atmosphere is at its strongest:

|   |   | And the knowledge | ooOo |
|---|---|---|---|
| 16 | Inside the hill on which you are sitting, | | OooO oOooOo |
|    | A moated fort hill, bigger than your house, | | oOoOO / OoooO |
| 18 | Failed to reach the picture. While your next moment, | | OoOoOo / OoOOo |
|    | Coming towards you like an infantryman | | OooOo ooOooO |
| 20 | Returning slowly out of no-man's-land, | | oOoOo OoOOO |
|    | Bowed under something, never reached you – | | OooOo / OoOo |

...

The second group of spondees follows in lines 17, 18 and 20, a 'fort hill' OO, the 'next moment' OOo, and is expanded to the molossus 'no-man's-land' OOO. They create emphasis and so does the adonii OooOo of lines (9), 10, 19, 21 – every time this salient figure occurs in the very beginning of a line, thus underlined. The adonii of lines 9–10 prepares for those of lines 19 and 21. The adonius is marked out by a certain energy, the dance rhythm swings and within this context it may force you into horror – this 'infantryman' may know about arriving deaths. The very last line 22 returns to the rhythm style that dominates in the first part of the poem, with many weaks together and a closeness to speech rhythm.

Varying stress ratios are important for the rhythmic impression. Style influences how to read. Speech style here is rather careless, and it calls upon the reader to increase the tempo, thereby not using some of the possible stresses. I have already pointed at the sharp contrasts in the line pair 8–9, which makes this passage a loaded one. In line 9, the first phrase is accentuated with the tense stress ratio of 1.7 ('Only a few weeks' OooOO), but the second phrase is extremely light with a value of 6 ('into his innocence' oooOoo). Another irregular passage follows with line 17:

|   |   | SSR |
|---|---|---|
| ... | | |
| A moated fort hill, bigger than your house, | oOoOO / OoooO | 1.7–2.5 |
| ... | | |

## Repetitions

Repetition is a main concept in versification. Many cases have met through this text. Repetition belongs to the right half of the brain, that is, it is not at first hand logical (Tsur 2017: 40). In Chapter 6, I connected repetition with one basic pattern of time – not the forward time arrow but the ever returning spiral time, that may be illustrated with the help of returning seasons and the lunar month.

All through this book I have emphasized that the repetitions of verse language are approximate. Even if the very element is exactly the same, the context has changed. The periodicity of spiral time constructs the model for approximate returns. Repetition occurs when new information meets an already familiar schema (Tsur 2017: 34).

Freud was interested in similarities – and repetitions are, of course, similarities. He distinguished between two kinds of thinking, according to similarity or according to succession that pursues causation – a more intellectual way to react. The two of them are named 'primary process' and 'secondary process' because they follow each other in the development of a child. The hungry child thinks, or rather feels, according to the primary process (similarity) and gets upset in front of anything that reminds him of – is similar to – a gruel bottle. When somewhat more mature, the child is able to notice causation and consecution (direction) in the secondary process. However, our dreams will always keep to the primary process and work with similarities and repetitions (Freud 1976; Lilja 1999: 44). This indicates that the primary process is always at work inside us.

According to Freud, similarity and repetition produce emotion. When transferred to the signification of sounds, similarity mixes and confuses the saying. Another psychoanalyst, Julia Kristeva, explains the repetitions in poetry with economy of desire (Kristeva 1980: 117). Psychoanalysis seems to agree with cognitive theory in looking at repetition as a method for building up strong emotion, even if they differ in the way they explain this phenomenon.

Twin pan balance implies repetition. To have a twin pan balance, something must be reiterated. The forward direction as well as the repetition are kinds of basic principles in the development of both society and nature. Culture is built on repeated behaviour as well as forward jumps of innovation (Spitzer 2002: 125) – new information and well-known schemas. That repetition is a main category in versification, as seen in Chapter 7 where I investigated cognitive economy. This involves modern free verse as well as metres.

In Chapter 6, I discussed some types of time that influence how people read poems. Nature seems to work in spirals, and one comes back to – approximately – the same position after some time (springtime arrives, new generations grow up, etc.). This model of time is periodic. Thinking of last springtime – or summer, or winter – the time in between shrinks considerably. In a text, an end rhyme brings the reader back to the first occurrence in a spatializing move that stops the forward reading direction and transforms a piece of text into one expanded moment. However, as was demonstrated in Chapter 7, complete similarity automatizes the reading – it spoils some text qualities. To maintain a signifying form, one must repeat it slightly differently; that is, one has to change the form a little bit to be able to communicate the same content (Danielsen 2006: 159; Spitzer 2002: 125). The similarity is approximate.

Poetry, here, has been defined as a text that is divided into short lines. The poet determines where to end the line, but in prose this will be decided by typographical circumstances. The short lines imply that one will meet a small pause – of about half a second – at every line ending. Surely, this must be the most ordinary repetition to appear in poems. Some poetry elaborates this kind of silence with strikingly short lines and much white paper around every line, but ordinary line lengths – as is the case in 'Perfect Light' – also produce pauses that determine the character of the text. The small silence that occurs every three seconds brings the line together, provides room for a completed gestalt and a full understanding of its significance (Nyberg and Sandell 2017: 78).

Balances hinder the time flow in a text. Repetition disturbs the basic forward movement, since it forces the reader to go back to the first occurrence, which makes the text in between ring in the reader's mind – even if this reaction might be subliminal. Repetition is a kind of diversion which creates tardy passages that are intended to vary the reading tempo.

In Hughes' poem, in addition to the repetition of the title that seems to keep the text together, another repetition is the eagerly reiterated 'daffodils':

>  There you are, in all your innocence,
> 2 Sitting among your daffodils, as in a picture
>  Posed as for the title: 'Innocence'.
> 4 Perfect light in your face lights it up
>  Like a daffodil. Like any one of those daffodils
> 6 It was to be your only April on earth
>  Among your daffodils.
>  …
> 12 …                    Like a daffodil
>  You turn your face down to her, saying something.
>  …

Line 5–7 contain three 'daffodils'; some of them could easily be replaced with a pronoun if one looks only at grammar. The protagonist is most determinedly compared with a daffodil, in terms of innocence, lighting and a short life. The flowers carry the first slight threat to the woman ('your only April'), a threat that will grow with every return and become a hurricane in the poem's last part with the entry of the infantryman. The repeated comparison with the flower stresses her fragility and her beauty.

The 'daffodils' of line 7 close the description of the main figure before her children are introduced, and the only thing to learn about her is this similarity with the flowers. The last repetition is one too many to be correct language – the beginning as well as the end of the same sentence accentuate the flowers (l. 5, 7). In the beginning and end, yes, like a twin pan.

Words, to some degree, change meaning when repeated, or produce extra significance – more significance and stronger feelings. The repeated elements colour one another – the moon in June will be a pale one. Also, the new context influences what is said. The first 'daffodil' of line 5 just recalls that in line 2, but the second (l. 5) takes over the described person, and the ungrammatical repetition of line 7 does so even more. The threat is strengthened when the recurrence of 'daffodils' (l. 7) cooperates with the sad prediction of line 6. In the next part, lines 7–14, the reader comes to know the protagonist only with the help of two images – the flower and the Madonna.

Emotion needs time and attention to expand. When the poem moves slowly, the reader is able to listen to their own reactions. This is one reason why repetitions add densification. Reader reactions shape rhythm when they block movements, which strengthens some elements while letting others pass. The slow parts are given emphasis in both thinking and feeling. The time that is needed is created with the help of divergence; that is, complications or diversions that prevent the automatization of ordinary speech and make poetic language something extra (Tsur 2008: 185ff.).

# 12

# Rhythm in modern poetry

## Rhythm is experience

In the nineteenth century, poems were mostly performed verbally. Poets read their work at receptions in cultural lounges. The versification means of tactus and end rhymes were necessary in such environments. To perceive the meaning, the listeners needed substantial tools for their reception process. However, around the year 1900, the lounges disappeared at the same time as printing costs substantially decreased. In this new situation, poets preferred to print and sell their books, and former listeners became silent readers. The tactus could be left aside, when silent reading offered other possibilities for understanding. It was now possible to go back through the text and return to previous passages when interpreting the text, in a so-called spatial reading. One could walk around in the text, so to speak, and go to-and-fro like walking in a room. This gave space for new, more sophisticated ways of versification.

Poetic rhythm takes place in perception. The acoustic and visual devices of a poem transform into rhythm when perceived by the reader. Rhythm schemas are perceptual entities that are triggered by means of versification, in line and phrase, like repetitions, caesuras, tactus, prolongations, and so on – salient gestalts at all levels. Rhythm is formed in a process, where reading adjusts the sounds of a poem. DIRECTION and BALANCE are two basic patterns in human perception, and they organize the perceptual impulses of a poem. However, both of them vary the deeper bodily experience of FORCE.

Acoustic registration differs a little from notations of what you really hear. The poet creates rhythms and figures out of speech rhythms, and the reader instinctively changes them into more distinct patterns. And, in the case of recitation, the listener sharpens the figures once more.

A poem consists of gestalts in varied sizes. Here I have differed between four levels of rhythm: phrase, line, stanza and the whole poem. Directions and balances work within them all, and rhythm on different levels clash as well as cooperate, as could be seen in the poem comments above. As a result, there will be different versions which leave room for different interpretations.

## Signification

The production of significance is, of course, influenced by form, acoustic qualities as well as visual ones. During the Baroque era, school books taught which feelings should cooperate with which qualities. In modern free verse, the relationship between form and meaning works more subtly. But even if the signification may be subliminal at first, one is able to trace its roots (Tsur 2012b).

Here, my primary interest has been sensorimotor experiences, biorhythms and the human body. That way, I have come close to the signification theories of Kandinsky – qualities such as the lightness and heaviness of weight, left and right, and quick and slow. Such aspects have turned out to have the ability to influence the semantic field of a word; to decide where to find the actual sense out of several possible nuances (Tynyanov [1924] 1981: 91–4). Details in shape may underline or remove significance, and connect or distinguish the elements of a line. Mostly, rhythms affect emotive signification – a direction may be aggressively energetic or depressingly slow. Rhythm cooperates with semantic meaning in most cases, but sometimes they oppose each other.

## Rhythm in modern free verse

Poetic rhythm arises when perceptual schemas are triggered by the devices of versification. The experience of rhythm is decided by a tension between cognitive factors and cultural conventions. The cognitive elements consist of experiences of balance, direction, force and movement. The cultural elements consist of historically developed patterns like verse patterns – such as those created by Sappho, Snorri Sturluson, Petrarcha, Mallarmé and others. Aesthetic rhythm arises when perceptual schemas are activated by the form elements of versification and specified with the help of, at first hand, biorhythms.

Above, I have stressed the influence of spatiality in the temporal flow of poetic rhythm. According to Jakobson, poetry is signified by repeated form elements. Every repetition points back to a previous moment in the text – the repetition directs the attention backwards. Tsur's process of back-structuring demonstrates how time moves when reading. Of course, the reading follows the time forward, but the form (as well as the message) could first be understood when the gestalt is closed in a returning movement of the attention. This will create an experience of going back or standing still, like one is able to in space but not in time. When reading poetry, one is allowed to stay in the moment, and the time arrow for once seems to have stopped its way – something that gives extra room for intensifying both thought and feeling. The time spiral makes a tense standstill.

I have argued that balance and direction are the key concepts here. Rhythm in poetry can be described as hierarchies of gestalts that are characterized by BALANCE and DIRECTION. In other words, poetic rhythm may consist of an interplay between direction – an urge to move forward, and balance – an impulse to stop time and rest. Poetic rhythm can be seen as a dialectic process between perceived direction and perceived balance within or between perceived gestalts.

Rhythm in an art work demonstrates a play with temporal and spatial proportions. The experience of limited movement seems to form the basis of any aesthetic rhythm. Rhythm in poetry can be understood as patterns of mobility within gestalts. Rising figures move forward with time, while falling rhythm departs from its focus.

Rhythm can also be defined as a balanced form on its way to tumble, where forces attack weights in order to threaten balances, thus creating directions within its gestalt. A good rhythm gives an impression of balance; however, not too stable. Slightly touching the limit of chaos gives rhythm that extra thrill.

BALANCE is the cognitive schema that is specific for works of art. Rhythm in an art work signifies the play between balance and the deviation from balance. Prose runs on with its weak gestalt borders, but poetry, with its strong gestalts, stops movements and repeats forms, making time pause in a string of magical moments. The impression of balance keeps the now, and accumulates time and attention. One seems to break free from the time arrow – forward directed time – and signification expands when time is slowing down. All the many movements in a poem bring its rhythms to life, but the pursuit of balance gives poetry that special feeling.

Balance implies repetition. Turning back in the text gives the reader the opportunity to expand the moment and keep its signification intact for many seconds in a kind of eternal now. Time seems to stand still just like a body in balance. The course of time seems to stop, allowing the reader to be aware of the text in between the two repeated expressions – both its form and its meaning. The now is expanded.

# References

Allen, G. W. (1975), *The New Walt Whitman Handbook*, New York: New York University Press.
Andrews, R. (2017), *A Prosody of Free Verse: Explorations in Rhythm*, London: Routledge.
Aristotle (1965), *The Poetics* [...], T. E. Page (ed.), London: Heinemann (Loeb Classical Library).
Arnheim, R. (1969), *Visual Thinking*, Berkeley, CA: University of California Press.
Arnheim, R. (1982), *The Power of the Centre: A Study of Composition in the Visual Arts*, rev. edn, Berkeley, CA: University of California Press.
Arnheim, R. (2004), *Art and Visual Perception: A Psychology of the Creative Eye*, exp. and rev. edn, Berkeley, CA: University of California Press.
Arnholtz, A. (1960), 'De Frie Vers' ['Free verse'], *Nysvenska studier* [*New Swedish Studies*], Uppsala: Appelbergs.
Ash, M. G. (1995), *Gestalt Psychology in German Culture, 1890–1967: Holism and the Quest for Objectivity*, Cambridge: Cambridge University Press.
Attridge, D. (1982), *The Rhythms of English Poetry*, London: Longman.
Attridge, D. (2012), 'The Case for the English Dolnik, or, How Not to Introduce Poetry', *Poetics Today*, 33: 1–26.
Attridge, D. (2013), *Moving Words: Forms of English Poetry*, Oxford: Oxford University Press.
Bassnett, S. (2005), *Sylvia Plath: An Introduction to the Poetry*, 2nd edn, London: Palgrave Macmillan.
Belfrage, S. (1941), *Die Entstehung der Freien Rhythmen*, Lund: K. Humanistiska vetenskapssamfundets i Lunds årsberättelse.
Booth, W. C. (1974), *A Rhetoric of Irony*, Chicago, IL: University of Chicago Press.
Bradley, S. (1939), 'The Fundamental Metrical Principle of Whitman's Poetry', *American Literature*, 10 (4): 437–59.
Brandt, P. A. and U. Cronquist (2019), *The Music of Meaning: Essays in Cognitive Semiotics*, Cambridge: Cambridge University Press.
Cable, T. (1974), *The Meter and Melody of Beowulf*, Urbana, IL: University of Illinois Press.
Chemi, T. (2016), 'The Experience of Flow in Artistic Creation', in L. Harmat et al. (eds), *Flow Experience: Empirical Research and Applications*, Berlin: Springer.
Cohen, L. (1972), *The Energy of Slaves*, Toronto: McClelland & Stewart.

Cooper, G. B. (1998), *Mysterious Music: Rhythm and Free Verse*, Stanford, CA: Stanford University Press.

Couper-Kuhlen, E. (1993), *English Speech Rhythm: Form and Function in Everyday Verbal Interaction*, Amsterdam: John Benjamins.

Creed, R. P. (1990), *Reconstructing the Rhythm of Beowulf*, Columbia, MO and London: University of Missouri Press.

Cureton, R. (1992), *Rhythmic Phrasing in English Verse*, London: Longman.

Danielsen, A. (2006), *Presence and Pleasure: The Funk Grooves of James Brown and Parliament*, Middletown, CT: Wesleyan University Press.

Eliot, T. S. (1917), 'Reflections on Vers Libre', *New Statesman*.

Eliot, T. S. (1930). *Ash-Wednesday*, London: Faber and Faber.

Eliot, T. S. ([1942] 1958), 'Poesins Musik' ['The Music in Poetry'], *Om Poesi* [*About Poetry*], Stockholm: Bonnier.

Elleström, L. (2010a), 'Iconicity as Meaning Miming Meaning and Meaning Miming Form', in J. Conradie (ed.), *Signergy*, Amsterdam: John Benjamins.

Elleström, L. (2010b), 'The Modalities of Media: A Model for Understanding Media Relations', in L. Elleström (ed.), *Media Borders, Multimodality and Intermediality*, Basingstoke: Palgrave Macmillan.

Elleström, L. (2017), 'Bridging the Gap Between Image and Metaphor through Cross-modal Iconicity: An Interdisciplinary Model', in A. Zirker et al. (eds), *Dimensions of Iconicity*, Amsterdam: De Gruyter.

Evans, S. (2016), '"Molpe" and Metrics in the Performance of Homer', unpublished manuscript.

Ferlinghetti, L. (1958), *A Coney Island of the Mind*, New York: New Directions.

Finch, A. (1993), *The Ghost of Meter: Culture and Prosody in American Free Verse*, Ann Arbor, MI: University of Michigan Press.

Fraisse, P. (1963), *The Psychology of Time*, New York: Harper & Row.

Freeman, M. H. (2002), 'The Body in the Word: A Cognitive Approach to the Shape of a Poetic Text', in E. Semino and J. Culpeper (eds), *Cognitive Stylistics*, Amsterdam: John Benjamins.

Freeman, M. H. (2008), 'Revisiting/Revisioning the Icon through Metaphor', *Poetics Today*, 29 (2): 353–70.

Freeman, M. H. (2009), 'Minding: Feeling, Form, and Meaning in the Creation of Poetic Iconicity', in G. Brône and J. Vandaele (eds), *Cognitive Poetics: Goals, Gains and Gaps*, Berlin and New York: De Gruyter.

Freeman, M. H. (2017), 'Toward a Theory of Poetic Iconicity: The Ontology of Semblance', in A. Zirker et al. (eds), *Dimensions of Iconicity*, Amsterdam: De Gruyter.

Freeman, M. H. (2020), *The Poem as Icon: A Study in Aesthetic Cognition*, Oxford: Oxford University Press.

Freud, S. (1976), *The Interpretation of Dreams*, Harmondsworth: Penguin.

Gallace, A. and C. Spence (2011), 'To what Extent do Gestalt Grouping Principles Influence Tactile Perception?', *Psychological Bulletin*, 137 (4): 538–61.

Gallagher, S. (2005), *How the Body Shapes the Mind*, Oxford: Oxford University Press.

Gärdenfors, P. (2006), *Den Meningssökande Människan [A Human Looking for Meaning]*, Stockholm: Natur & Kultur.

Gasparov, M. L. (1996), *A History of European Versification*, Oxford: Clarendon Press.

Gibbs, R. W. Jr. (2005), *Embodiment and Cognitive Science*, Cambridge: Cambridge University Press.

Grosser, E. J. (2017), 'A Cognitive Poetics Approach to the Problem of Biblical Hebrew Poetic Lineation: Perception-oriented Lineation of David's Lament in 2 Samuel 1:19–27', *Hebrew Studies*, 58: 173–98.

Grosser, E. J. (2023), *Unparalleled Poetry: A Cognitive Approach to the Free-Rhythm Verse of the Hebrew Bible*, New York: Oxford University Press.

Hampe, B. (2005), 'Image Schemas in Cognitive Linguistics: Introduction', in B. Hampe (ed.), *From Perception to Meaning: Image Schemas in Cognitive Linguistics*, Berlin: De Gruyter.

Hancil, S. and D. Hirst, eds (2013), *Prosody and Iconicity*, Amsterdam: Benjamins.

Hanslick, E. ([1854] 1955), *Om det Sköna i Musiken [Vom Musikalisch-Schönen]*, Uppsala: Schismen.

Hartman, C. O. (1980), *Free Verse: An Essay on Prosody*, Princeton, NJ: Princeton University Press.

Heaney, S. (1969), *Door into the Dark*, London: Faber and Faber.

Heaney, S. (1984), *Station Island*, London: Faber and Faber.

Hellmuth, H.-H. (1973), *Metrische Erfindung und metrische Theorie bei Klopstock*, München: Fink.

Hopsch, L. (2008), *Rytmens Estetik, Formens Kraft [The Aesthetics of Rhythm, the Force of Form]*, PhD diss., Chalmers University, Gothenburg.

Hopsch, L. and Eva Lilja (2007), 'Principles of Rhythm. Temporal and Spatial Aspects', in J. Arvidson (ed.), *Changing Borders: Contemporary Positions in Intermediality*, Lund: Intermedia Studies Press.

Hopsch, L. and Eva Lilja (2013), 'Rhythm and Balance in Sculpture and Poetry', in J. H. Hoogstad and B. S. Pedersen (eds), *Off Beat: Pluralizing Rhythm*, Amsterdam and New York: Rodopi.

Hopsch, L. and Eva Lilja (2017), 'Embodied Rhythm in Space and Time: A Poem and a Sculpture', *Style*, 51 (4): 413.

Hoy, D. C. (2009), *The Time of Our Lives: A Critical History of Temporality*, Cambridge, MA: MIT Press.

Hrushovski, B. (1954), 'On Free Rhythms in Modern Yiddish Poetry', in U. Weinreich (ed.), *The Field of Yiddish: Studies in Yiddish Language, Folklore and Literature*, New York: The Linguistic Circle of New York.

Hrushovski, B. (1960), 'On Free Rhythms in Modern Poetry: Preliminary Remarks toward a Critical Theory of their Structures and Functions', in T. A. Sebeok (ed.), *Style in Language*, Cambridge, MA: MIT Press.

Hrushovski, B. (1980), 'The Meaning of Sound Patterns in Poetry', *Poetics Today*, 2 (1): 39–56.

Hughes, T. (1998), *Birthday Letters*, London: Faber and Faber.

Jakobson, R. (1960), 'Linguistics and Poetics', in T. A. Sebeok (ed.), *Style in Language*, Cambridge, MA: MIT Press.

Jakobson, R. and L. Waugh (1979), *The Sound Shape of Language*, Brighton: Harvester Press.

Jansson, M. (1991), *Tradition och Förnyelse: Den Svenska Introduktionen av T.S. Eliot [Tradition and Innovation: The Swedish Introduction of T.S. Eliot]*, PhD diss., Gothenburg University, Gothenburg.

Johnson, M. (1987), *The Body in the Mind: The Bodily Basis of Signification, Imagination and Reason*, Chicago, IL: University of Chicago Press.

Johnson, M. (2007), *The Meaning of the Body: Aesthetics of Human Understanding*, Chicago, IL: University of Chicago Press.

Johnson, M. (2018), *The Aesthetics of Meaning and Thought: The Bodily Roots of Philosophy, Science, Morality, and Art*, Chicago, IL: University of Chicago Press.

Johnson, M. and T. Rohrer (2007), 'We are Live Creatures: Embodiment, American Pragmatism, and the Cognitive Organism', in J. Zlatev et al. (eds), *Body, Language, and Mind, vol. 1*, Berlin and New York: De Gruyter.

Kandinsky, W. (1912), *Über das Geistige in der Kunst*, München: Piper.

Kandinsky, W. (1916), *Om konstnären [About the Artist]*, Stockholm: Gummeson.

Kandinsky, W. ([1928] 1955), *Punkt und Linie zu Fläche: Beitrag zur Analyse der malerischen Elemente*, 10th edn, Bern: Benteli Verlag.

Kjørup, F. (2003), *Sprog versus Sprog: Mod en Versets Poetik [Language versus Language: Against a Poetics of Verse]*, Copenhagen: Museum Tusculanum.

Kjørup, F. (2008), 'Grammetics and Cognitive Semantics: Metaphorical and Force Dynamic Aspects of Verse-Syntax-Counterpoint', *Cognitive Semiotics*, 2: 83–101.

Kristeva, J. (1980), *Desire in Language: A Semiotic Approach to Literature and Art*, New York: Columbia University Press.

Kristeva, J. ([1974] 1984), *Revolution in Poetic Language*, New York: Columbia University Press.

Kristeva, J. ([1987] 1989), *Black Sun: Depression and Melancholia*, New York: Columbia University Press.

Kruckenberg, A. and G. Fant (1993), 'Iambic versus Trochaic Patterns in Poetry Reading', *Nordic Prosody*, VI: 123–35, Stockholm: Almqvist & Wiksell International.

Kubovy, M. and D. van Valkenburg (2006), 'Auditory and Visual Objects', in M. Bertamini and M. Kubovy (eds), *Human Perception*, Aldershot: Ashgate.

Kühl, O. (2003), *Improvisation og tanke [Improvisation and Thought]*, Copenhagen: Basilisk.

Kühl, O. (2007), *Musical Semantics*, Bern: Peter Lang.

Lakoff, G. and M. Johnson (1980), *Metaphors We Live By*, Chicago, IL: University of Chicago Press.

Lakoff, G. and M. Johnson (1999), *Philosophy in the Flesh: The Embodied Mind and Its Challenge to Western Thought*, New York: Basic Books.

Lauvstad, H. (1993), *Moderne sonetter: En studie av form og funksjon i skandinavisk sonettdiktning etter 1940* [*Modern sonnets*], Oslo: Solum.

Lilja, Efva (2006), *Movement as the Memory of the Body*, Stockholm: University College of Dance.

Lilja, Eva (1999), 'Dikters Ljudbild' ['The Sound Picture of the Poem'], in Eva Lilja and M. Nordman (eds), *Bidrag till en Nordisk Metrik* [*A Contribution to Nordic Metrics, vol. 1*], Gothenburg: Centre for Studies in Metrics.

Lilja, Eva (2003), 'The Staves of Alliteration and the Prominences of "Knittel": A Contribution to the Problem of the Scandinavian Four Beat Line', *Jahrbuch für Internationale Germanistik*, XXXV: 1.

Lilja, Eva (2006), *Svensk Metrik* [*Swedish Metrics*], Stockholm: The Swedish Academy.

Lilja, Eva (2007), 'Den besynnerliga metern' ['This Peculiar Metre'], in S. Ekman (ed.), *Den Litterära Textens Förändringar* [*Changes of the Literary Text*], Stockholm/Stehag: Brutus Östling.

Lilja, Eva (2014), *Poesiens Rytmik: En Essä om Form och Betydelse* [*Rhythm in Poetry: An Essay about Form and Signification*], Knopparp: Ariel.

Lilja Norrlind, E. (1981), *Studier i svensk fri vers: Den fria versen hos Vilhelm Ekelund och Edith Södergran* [*Studies in Swedish Free Verse*], PhD diss., Gothenburg University, Gothenburg.

Linde, L. (1974), *Perception of Poetic Rhythm*, PhD diss., Stockholm University, Stockholm.

Livius, Titus (1924), Books V, VI and VII, Cambridge, MA: Harvard University Press (Loeb Classical Library).

Lonsdale, S. H. (1992), *Dance and Ritual Play in Greek Religion*, Baltimore, MD: Johns Hopkins University Press.

Lotman, J. (1972), *Die Struktur literarischer Texte*, München: Fink.

Maas, P. (1962), *Greek Metre*, Oxford: Clarendon Press.

Madsen, P. (1990), 'Betydningsbegrebet i Aestetisk Analyse: Hinsides Semiosis' ['The Concept of Signification in Aesthetic Analysis: On the Other Side of Semiosis'], *Tidskrift för Litteraturvetenskap* [*Journal of Comparative Literature*], 4: 26–34.

Malmström, S. (1971), *Stil och versform i svensk poesi 1900–1926* [*Style and Versification in Swedish Poetry 1900–1926*], Stockholm: The Swedish Academy.

Mannerheim, A. (1991), 'Mäta och beräkna i talad text: Metodik och fynd' ['Measure and Calculate in Spoken Text: Methods and Findings'], in *Vers-Mått* [*Metres and Measures*], Gothenburg: Centre for Metric Studies.

Merleau-Ponty, M. ([1945] 2002), *Phenomenology of Perception*, London: Routledge.

Meyer, L. B. (1956), *Emotion and Meaning in Music*, Chicago, IL: University of Chicago Press.

Miller, G. A. (1970), *The Psychology of Communication*, Harmondsworth: Penguin.

Muldoon, M. S. (2006), *Tricks of Time: Bergson, Merleau-Ponty and Ricœur in Search of Time, Self and Meaning*, Pittsburgh, PA: Duquesne University Press.

Muldoon, P. (2010), *Maggot*, New York: Farrar, Straus and Giroux.

Murray, D. J. (1995), *Gestalt Psychology and the Cognitive Revolution*, New York: Harvester.

Nänny, M. (1986), 'Iconicity in Literature', *Word & Image*, 2 (3): 199–208.

Nänny, M. (2001), 'Iconic Functions of Long and Short Lines', in O. Fischer and M. Nänny (eds), *The Motivated Sign: Iconicity in Language and Literature*, 2nd edn, Amsterdam: John Benjamins.

Nässén, E. (2000), '*Ett yttre tecken på en inre känsla*': Studier i barockens musikaliska och svenska gestik ['A Visible Sign of an Inner Feeling.' Studies in the Musical Gesture of the Swedish Baroque], PhD diss., Gothenburg University, Gothenburg.

Neisser, U. (1976), *Cognition and Reality: Principles and Implications of Cognitive Psychology*, San Francisco, CA: Freeman.

Nordman, M. (1987), *Rytm och Balans i Svensk Prosatext* [*Rhythm and Balance in Swedish Prose Texts*], Umeå: Nordsvenska.

Nöth, W. (2001), 'Semiotic Foundations of Iconicity in Language and Literature', in O. Fischer and M. Nänny (eds), *The Motivated Sign*, Amsterdam: John Benjamins.

Nyberg, F. (2013), *Hur låter dikten?* [*What is the Sound of Poetry?*], PhD diss., Gothenburg University, Gothenburg.

Nyberg, F. and S. Sandell (2017), *Plötsligt Infinner sig en Oro: Essäer om Paus och Tystnad.* [*Suddenly There is a Disturbance: Essays about Pause and Silence*], Gothenburg: Autor.

Olsson, C. (1993), *Dansföreställningar: Dansestetiska Problem i Historisk Belysning och Speglade i Två Dansverk* [*Dance Performances: Aesthetic Problems of Dance in Historic Perspective*], PhD diss., Lund University, Lund.

Ong, W. J. ([1982] 2002), *Orality and Literacy: The Technologizing of the Word*, London: Taylor & Francis.

Otterloo, G. (1982), *Het Achterberg-sonnet: Bijdrage tot de interpretatie van Achterbergs sonnetten*, PhD diss., Gothenburg University, Gothenburg.

Perloff, M. (1999), *The Poetics of Indeterminacy: Rimbaud to Cage*, Evanston, IL: Northwestern University Press.

Persinger, M.A. (1987), *Neuropsychological Bases of God Beliefs*, New York: Praeger.

Piaget, J. ([1936] 1953), *Origins of Intelligence in Children*, New York: International Universities Press.

Plath, S. (1965), *Ariel*, London: Faber and Faber.

Plath, S. (1971), *Winter Trees*, London: Faber and Faber.

Plato (1939), *Cratylus*, Cambridge, MA: Harvard University Press (Loeb Classical Library).

Plato ([1926] 1952), *Laws*, London: Heinemann (Loeb Classical Library).

Pöppel, E. (2004), 'Lost in Time: A Historical Frame, Elementary Processing Units and the 3-Second Window', *Acta Neurobiologiae Experimentalis*, 64 (3): 295–301.

Pourcel, S. (2010), 'Motion: A Conceptual Typology', in V. Evans and P. Chilton (eds), *Language, Cognition and Space: The State of the Art and New Directions*, London: Equinox Publishing.

Quintilianus (1922), *The Institutio Oratoria*, vol. IV, Cambridge, MA: Cambridge University Press (Loeb Classical Library).

Raven, D. S. ([1962] 1998), *Greek Metre*, Bristol: Bristol Classical.

Ricœur, P. ([1985] 1990), *Time and Narrative*, vol. 3, Chicago, IL: University of Chicago Press.

Rohrer, T. (2005), 'Image Schemata in the Brain', in B. Hampe (ed.), *From Perception to Meaning: Image Schemas in Cognitive Linguistics*, Berlin: De Gruyter.

Schrott, R. and A. Jacobs (2011), *Gehirn und Gedicht. Wie wir unsere Wirklichkeiten konstruieren*, München: Hanser.

Sexton, A. (1969), *Love Poems*, Boston: Houghton Mifflin Co.

Sexton, A. (1974), *The Death Notebooks*, Boston: Houghton Mifflin Co.

Smith, B. H. (1968), *Poetic Closure: A Study of How Poems End*, Chicago, IL: University of Chicago Press.

Snyder, E. D. (1930), *Hypnotic Poetry: A Study of Trance-inducing Technique in Certain Poems and its Literary Significance*, Philadelphia, PA: University of Pennsylvania Press.

Sonesson, G. (2007), 'From the Signification of Embodiment to the Embodiment of Signification: A Study in Phenomenological Semiotics', in T. Ziemke (ed.), *Body, Language and Mind, vol. 1: Embodiment*, Berlin: De Gruyter.

Spitzer, M. (2002), *Musik im Kopf: Hören, Musizieren, Verstehen und Erleben im neuralen Netzwerk*, Stuttgart: Schattauer.

Starr, G. (2013), *Feeling Beauty: The Neuroscience of Aesthetic Experience*, Cambridge, MA: MIT Press.

Stougaard Pedersen, B. (2008), *Lyd, Litteratur og Musik: Gestus i Kunstoplevelsen* [*Sound, Literature, and Music: Gesture in the Experience of Art*], Aarhus: Aarhus University Press.

Talmy, L. (2000), *Toward a Cognitive Semantics*, Cambridge, MA: MIT Press.

Trevarthen, C. (2009), 'Human Biochronology: On the Source and Functions of "Musicality"', in R. Haas and V. Brandes (eds), *Music that Works: Contributions of Biology, Neurophysiology, Psychology, Sociology, Medicine and Musicology*, Wien: Springer.

Tsur, R. (1992), *What Makes Sound Patterns Expressive? The Poetic Mode of Speech Perception*, Durham, NC: Duke University Press.

Tsur, R. (2003), *On the Shore of Nothingness: Space, Rhythm, and Semantic Structure in Religious Poetry and its Mystic-secular Counterpart. A Study in Cognitive Poetics*, Exeter: Imprint Academic.

Tsur, R. (2008), *Toward a Theory of Cognitive Poetics*, 2nd edn, Brighton: Sussex Academic Press.

Tsur, R. (2009), 'Aesthetic Qualities as Structural Resemblance: Divergence and Perceptual Forces in Poetry', Toronto. Available online: www.tau.ac.il/~tsurxx/Structural_Resemblance/within_thine_own.html (accessed 1 June 2022).

Tsur, R. (2011), 'Some Remarks on the Nature of Trochees and Iambs and their Relationship to Other Metres', *PSYART*, Gainsville, FL: University of Florida.

Tsur, R. (2012a), *Poetic Rhythm: Structure and Performance: An Empirical Study in Cognitive Poetics*, 2nd edn, Brighton: Sussex Academic Press.

Tsur, R. (2012b), *Playing by Ear and the Tip of the Tongue: Precategorial Information in Poetry*, Amsterdam/Philadelphia: John Benjamins.

Tsur, R. (2017), *Poetic Conventions as Cognitive Fossils*, Oxford: Oxford University Press.

Tsur, R. and C. Gafni (2022), *Sound-Emotion Interaction in Poetry: Rhythm, Phonemes, Voice Quality*, Amsterdam: John Benjamins.

Turner, F. and E. Pöppel (1983), 'The Neural Lyre: Poetic Meter, the Brain, and Time', *Poetry*, 142 (5): 277–309.

Turner, M. (1996), *The Literary Mind*, New York: Oxford University Press.

Tynyanov, Y. ([1924] 1981), *The Problem of Verse Language*, Ann Arbor, MI: Ardis.

Varela, F. J., E. Thompson and E. Rosch (1993), *The Embodied Mind: Cognitive Science and Human Experience*, rev. edn, Cambridge, MA: MIT Press.

Wagenknecht, C. (1971), *Weckherlin und Opitz: Zur Metrik der deutschen Renaissancepoesie*, München: Beck.

West, M. L. (1982), *Greek Metre*, Oxford: Clarendon Press.

Wood, D. (1992), *A Critical Study of the Birth Imagery of Sylvia Plath, American Poet 1932-1963*, Lewiston, NY: Edwin Mellen Press.

# Index

'13' (Ferlinghetti) 65–9, 70

accent-syllabic versification *see* accentual-syllabic verse
accentual rhythm 115
accentual verse/versification 5–7, 19, 20, 21
accentual-syllabic verse 6–7
acoustic direction 59
acoustic weight 59, 140
adonius 31, 143, 147
aeolic poetry 7
alexandrine 19, 20–1, 29, 118
alliteration 30, 108–9, 114, 132
alternation
    cognitive economy 89, 95, 96, 97
    free verse definitions 8–9
    patterns of culture 115
    poem in the body 106–8
    rhythm and significance 43, 47
ambiguity 36, 97, 128
amphibrachs 34–8, 75–6
amplitude 127, 129
amygdala 101
anapaests
    cognitive economy 95
    cognitive versification theory 71
    direction 127–9, 131–2
    European versification studies 31
    Homer 2
    patterns of culture 121–2
    rhythmic gestalt 31, 32–6
ancient Greece *see* Old Greek poetry
antepenultima 134
anticipation *see* prolongation
Antique type of free verse 7, 93, 99
antispast *see* colon
Aristotle 78–9
Arnheim, Rudolf 29, 52–3, 64, 128
'Ash Wednesday' (Eliot) 90–7
associations, multisensory associations 39–40, 51, 113

assonance 23, 24, 108–9
Attridge, Derek 4–6, 8, 11, 13
    levels and times 84
    patterns of culture 115–16, 123
    poem in the body 101
    rhythm and significance 43
    rhythmic gestalt 30
audibility, audible 52
avant-garde versification 7, 8, 22
axis 107, 108–9, 142
axis balance 141–5

bacchius *see* colon
back-structuring 29, 107–8
backwards 3–4, 153
    balance 139, 143, 144
    direction 128–9, 133
    levels and times 81–2, 84, 85
    rhythmic gestalt 29
    temporal and spatial rhythms 56
balance 2, 3–4, 9–10, 151–3
    cognitive versification theory 70–1, 72
    direction 125, 127–8, 135–6
    how to 141–7
    levels and times 78–9, 84, 85
    patterns in culture 113
    poem in the body 107, 108–12
    rhythm and significance 39
    rhytmic gestalt 34–5
    verse systems/principles of rhythm 25
    in versification 139–50
    *see also* repetitions
BALANCE schema 64–5, 67–70, 72, 111
ballads 20, 91, 106
Baroque era 113, 152
basal ganglia 101
beat 5, 17, 19, 30, 32, 43, 46, 93, 101, 103, 105, 115, 116
*Beowulf* 20, 114–16, 123
Bible 7, 8, 123–4, 136
biorhythms 41–2, 45–7, 152
    cognitive versification theory 65, 74

levels and times 84
patterns of culture 123–4
poem in the body 101–12
*Birthday Letters* (Hughes) 141–7, 149–50
blending 21, 44
blockage *see* FORCE schema
Boccioni, Umberto 136–8, 139, 140
body rhythms 46, 106
Book of Psalms 8
breath interval, breathing 103

Cabaré Voltaire 8, 22
cadence 11, 13
caesura 21, 29, 42–3, 93–4, 114, 151
*Canzoniere* (Petrarcha) 117
Carmen Olsson 2–3, 9–10
  balance 145
  direction 128–30
  poem in the body 109, 111
  rhythm and significance 46–7
  verse systems/principles of rhythm 17–18
categorization, delayed categorization 85, 97, 98
Chaucer, Geoffrey 115
Chinese syllabomelodic verse 17
choriamb 31, 65, 68, 78
clock time/scientific time 56, 82–4, 131
closure 36–8
cognitive economy 89–99
cognitive metaphor 56, 125, 143
cognitive patterns 53, 124
cognitive psychology 89–90
cognitive schema 54, 63–4, 69
  nature of 64–7
  *see also* BALANCE; DIRECTION; FORCE
cognitive subconscious 65, 102
cognitive versification theory 63–74
Cohen, Leonard 77–81, 84–6, 122
colon 2, 23–4, 30–1, 37, 91, 146–7
'Composition 8' (Kandinsky) 41
compulsion
  and diversion 125–8
  *see also* FORCE schema
Concretism 22
*A Coney Island of the Mind* (Ferlinghetti) 65–9
continuity, law of 28, 29–30

convention 42–3, 113–14
conversational style 91–2
cooperation of modalities 62
counterforce *see* FORCE schema
cretic(i) 23–5, 43, 84, 143
Cureton, Richard 4–5, 6, 13, 14
  direction 128
  levels and times 75–6, 84
  poem in the body 101, 107–8
  rhythmic gestalt 28–9
  temporality 52
cyclical time 83

dactyl 14, 31, 34, 56, 59, 61
Dada movement, performance 2, 7, 8, 22, 43
dance, dancing 109–11
  *see also* Carmen Olsson; walking
Davis, Miles 126
deautomatization 97
deixis 131
Democritus 9
'Development of a Bottle in Space' (Boccioni) 139, 140
device 2, 4, 6, 7, 11, 151
  cognitive economy 90–1, 92, 94, 95
  cognitive versification theory 63
  direction 126, 127, 131, 133
  levels and times 79
  patterns of culture 118, 122
  poem in the body 104, 105–6
  rhythm and significance 42
  rhythmic gestalt 35
  temporal and spatial rhythms 52
  verse systems/principles of rhythm 22, 24
  *see also* enjambment; flow; tactus
diagonal 60, 61, 62
diagram 44, 45, 69, 128
dictums 98
digital reading 104
direction 3–4, 6, 9–10, 13, 17, 151–3
  BALANCE schema 64–5, 67–70, 72, 111
  balance 139, 140
  cognitive economy 96–7
  cognitive versification theory 67–8, 70–1
  compulsion and diversion 125–8

# Index

diagonal 60, 61, 62
enjambment 133–5
    flow 136–8
    levels and times 79, 80–4, 86
    patterns of culture 113
    poem in the body 107, 109, 111
    promenade metaphors 125–6
        reading direction 3, 56, 71, 129, 133, 149
    rhythm and significance 39, 40, 43, 47–9
    rhythmic gestalt 28–9, 35, 37–8
    rising/falling rhythm 128–33
    temporal and spatial rhythms 55–62
    verse systems/principles of rhythm 24
    *see also* backwards; forward, forwardness
DIRECTION schema 64–5, 67–70
diversion 70–1, 126–8, 131–3, 149–50
doggerel verse 115–16
*dolnik* 5, 123
dynamic rhythm 17–19, 69, 103, 116
dynamic tensions 54

echo memory 46, 103, 105
Eddaic forms 7
eight-syllable lines 20
Eliot, T.S. 90–7
embodiment 65, 103–4
    *see also* biorhythms; poem in the body
emotion 3–4, 5
    balance 148, 150
    biorhythms 101, 111
    cognitive economy 96–7
        signification 97–8
    levels and times 78
    patterns of culture 113
    repetitions 148–50
    rhythm and significance 39–40, 44, 47
    rhythmic gestalt 31–2
end-stopped lines 91, 93, 94–5
*The Energy of Slaves* (Cohen) 77–81, 84–6
England 115, 117
English disyllabic metre 21
English iambic pentameter 21, 42–3, 103–4, 118
enjambment 7, 13–14
    cognitive versification theory 71
    direction 126, 133–5
    rhythm and significance 48
    rhythmic gestalt 31, 33–7
    rising/falling rhythm 128–9, 130
    temporal and spatial rhythms 59
    verse systems/principles of rhythm 22–4
epitrite 31, 95, 96
equivalence 4
    balance 143, 145
    direction 128
    levels and times 83, 85
    rhythmic gestalt 38
ethos 61
expression(ism) 34, 39–40, 85–6, 91, 97–8, 107–8
expressivity 123–4
extention *see* prolongation

facsimile 66, 70
falling rhythm, falling tactus 56, 71, 84, 128–33, 153
Ferlinghetti, Lawrence 65–9, 70, 143
Finnish *rune metre* 132
flow 13, 18–19, 126, 131, 136–8, 153
    balance 146, 149
    levels and times 85
    rhythm and significance 47
    *see also* direction
focus
    focus point 84, 125
    phrasal focus 58
force 10, 17, 150, 152
    balance 140
    cognitive economy 95, 97–8
    direction 133
    enjambment 133
    levels and times 84
    patterns of culture 113
    rhythm and significance 43–4, 47–8
    rhythmic gestalt 36–7
    temporal and spatial rhythms 59
    *see also* BALANCE schema
FORCE schema 68–72, 125–8, 133, 135, 140, 151
form/meaning 73, 136, 137
    background murmur 72
    Eddaic forms 7
    measured 5

Petrarchan sonnets 40–5, 117, 118
tactility, tactile 53
forward, forwardness 2, 3–4, 10, 125–38, 153
    balance 139, 143, 148–9
    cognitive versification theory 64–5, 71
    levels and times 78–86
    patterns of culture 116–17, 120–2
    poem in the body 107, 109–10, 111
    rhythm and significance 40, 43–4, 45, 47–9
    rhythmic gestalt 33–8
    temporal and spatial rhythms 55–6, 59, 61–2
*Four Quartets* (Eliot) 91–2
four-beat measure 5, 7, 17, 20–2, 29–30
    cognitive economy 90, 91–7, 99
    cognitive versification theory 65–6
    patterns of culture 115–16, 118, 123
    poem in the body 103, 104, 106
    rhythm and significance 42–3
free verse 23, 152–4
    reading 87–154
Freeman, Margaret 21, 39, 44, 72–4, 109
French poetry
    eight-syllable lines 20
    medieval 42–3
    sonnets 118
    syllabic verse, syllabism 20, 21, 115
    *see also* alexandrine
Freud, Sigmund 148
'The Fury of Rain Storms' (Sexton) 31–8
future 81–2

Gärdenfors, Peter 54–5, 126
Gasparov, Mihail 5–6, 13, 17, 19–20, 115
'Gelb – Rot – Blau' (Kandinsky) 54–7
Germanic poetry/language 20, 22, 30–1, 37, 115, 116
    medieval accentual versification 19
gestalt 3–4, 5, 9–10, 151–2, 153
    balance 139, 142, 149
    cognitive economy 89–91, 93, 95–9
    direction 125, 127, 128, 129, 133–5
    patterns of culture 113–16
    poem in the body 101–5, 107–8
    strong and weak 99
    *see also* poetic gestalt

gestalt laws 28–9, 89–90
gestalt level 142
gestalt pressure 90, 115
gestalt psychology 5, 89–90
Gestalt school of psychology 28–9
gesture 40
Gibbs, Raymond 63, 65–6, 74
goal *see* prolongation
Goethe, Johann Wolfgang von 94
good gestalt, law of 28–9
grammar 119, 121, 127–8, 133–4
gravity 102, 128–33
Greek poetry 19–20, 30–1, 37
Grosser, Emilou 136
ground surface, *Grund Fläche* 56
grouping, grouping principles 17, 28–9

haiku 42
Heaney, Seamus 40–5, 104, 105–6
Heine, Heinrich 7, 30, 91
*hendekasillaba* 104, 113–14
hexameter 19–20, 29, 42, 113
*Hildebrandslied* fragments 20
hippocampus 101
Homer 2
Hughes, Ted 141–7, 149–50
hypnosis 99, 105

iambic pentameter 21, 42–3, 103–4, 118
iambs/iambic poetry 14
    cognitive economy 95
    cognitive versification theory 71
    direction 129, 130–1
    levels and times 80–1, 86
    patterns of culture 115, 116–17, 118
    poem in the body 103–4, 108
    rhythm and significance 45, 49
    rhythmic gestalt 31, 32, 33–6
    temporal and spatial rhythms 49, 56
    verse systems/principles of rhythm 17–18, 21
iconicity, icon 41–2, 43–5
    diagrammatic icon 45
        biorhythms 45–6
    rhythm and significance 43–5
image *see* semiotics
image schema *see* cognitive schema
imagery, multisensory imagery 51

imagined time 84–5
imagism, imagists 91–2
imbalance 9–10, 59–60, 125, 139, 143
incantations 43
index 131
intermedia perspectives 51–62
intervals 103–5
intonation curves 8, 29, 30, 107
intonation phrase 30, 104, 114, 123, 136
ionic 23–4, 33–4, 68, 80, 116–17
irony, irony marker 79–81, 122
isomorphism 43, 45
Isou, Isidore 22

Jakobson, Roman 38, 85, 153
   *see also* equivalence
Johnson, Mark 63–72, 104, 127, 128

*The Kalevala* 132
Kandinsky, Wassily 41, 53, 54–62, 152
King James Bible *see* Bible
Klopstock, Friedrich Gottlieb 7, 30–1, 94
Knowles, Gerry 134
Kristeva, Julia 148
Kühl, Ole 73, 126

language materialism 43
late peaking 134
laws of gestalt 28–9, 89–90
*The Laws* (Plato) 9
*Leaves of Grass* (Whitman) 138
length (syllables) 21, 31, 37, 48, 94, 95, 116, 121, 127, 128, 129, 134, 135, 140
Lettrism 22
levels 75–86
lexical meaning 39, 43, 49, 74
line 47, 75–6, 81, 142–3, 151–2
   patterned line 27–30
line break 7
   balance 142
   cognitive versification theory 71
   direction 127–8, 131, 133–4
   levels and times 79
   poem in the body 104, 107–8
   rhythm and significance 44, 48
   rhythmic gestalt 30, 31, 34, 37
   temporal and spatial rhythms 59

line direction 59
line lengths 144, 146
line schema 118, 122
lineation 22, 44, 133
line-break pause 134
Livius 118–23
*ljóðahattr* 115
long syllables 31, 37, 113
long-term memory 40, 73–4, 103–4, 105, 109
Lotman, Yuri 4
'The Love Song of J. Alfred Prufrock' (Eliot) 92

Mallarmé, Stéphane 152
marked, unmarked 131
materiality, signification of 39–42
measured forms 5
measure 19–20, 31, 144, 146
   alexandrine 19, 20–1, 29, 118
   domination of tactus 116
   eight-syllable lines 20
   English iambic pentameter 21, 42–3, 103–4, 118
   hexameter 19–20, 29, 42, 113
   sonnets 113–14, 117–23
   speech rhythm 123
memory 73–4, 81–2, 103
   echo memory 46, 103, 105
   enjambment 133
   *see also* long-term memory; short-term memory
Merleau-Ponty, Maurice 40, 65, 81, 111–12
metaphor *see* semiotics
metre 4, 7, 18–20, 21, 104
   balance 148
   patterns of culture 113–14, 115, 116, 117, 118
   rising/falling rhythm 132–3
   *rune metre* 132
   stress-timed metre 115
   *see also* tactus
minding 72
mixed rhythm 23, 24, 25, 42, 95, 121–2
modality 53, 62
   *see also* premodality
mode 9, 33, 73

modern sonnets 117–18
modernism 7, 23, 123–4
modern(ist) free verse 20, 21, 152–4
Modernist poetry 20
molossus 31, 33, 37, 44, 68, 69, 78, 80, 84, 86, 93, 94, 95, 99, 107, 109, 143, 147
motor imagery 51, 101
motor skills 63, 65, 102
motor systems 101, 102
*mousikē* 1–14, 51, 111
*Moving Words* (Attridge) 101
Muldoon, Paul 117, 118–23
'The Music in Poetry' (Eliot) 91

Nänny, Max 41, 44
narrative 126
neurological levels of embodying 65
neurology 5, 45, 104
*Niebelungenlied* 115
'Night Drive' (Heaney) 40–5
nursery rhymes 20
Nyberg, Fredrik 52, 149

octet 117, 121, 122
Old Greek poetry 22–4, 94
    adonius/colon 2, 23–4, 30–1, 37, 91, 146–7
    quantitative metre 19–20
Old Norse poetry 20, 30, 37, 115, 123–4
    see also Beowulf
oral poetry 114
orality 1
orbitofrontal cortex 101
Otfried 20, 115

paeon 48, 49, 76, 96
parallelism 8, 91, 139
paronomasia 11, 91
pattern conception 47
patterned line 27–30
patterns/patterning 1–2, 37, 40, 73, 95
    cognitive economy 89–99
    cognitive versification theory 63–6, 70
    of culture 113–24
    free verse definitions 7, 8
    levels and times 78–9, 81–2

Old Greek poetry 2, 22–4, 30–1, 37, 91, 94
Old Norse poetry 20, 30, 37, 115, 123–4
poem in the body 101, 103–4, 105, 107, 109–11
rhythm and significance 40, 43–4, 46–8
rhythmic gestalt 30–1
    closure 36–7
    patterned line 27–30
    temporal and spatial rhythms 52–4, 56, 61, 62
verse systems/principles of rhythm 19–25
see also balance; direction
pauses 39, 41, 134
see also line break
Peirce, Carles S. 44, 64
pentameter 90, 92–5, 99, 104
see also iambic pentameter
perception 1–2, 9, 13, 151
    cognitive economy 89–90
    cognitive versification theory 63–4, 65, 72–4
    poem in the body 101–4, 110, 111
    precategorical information, perception 72–4
    premodality 52–4, 73–4
    rhythm and significance 39–40
    rhythmic gestalt 28, 30
    temporal and spatial rhythms 51, 52–5
perceptual schema 63, 152
'Perfect Light' (Hughes) 141–7, 149–50
performance
    Dada movement, performances 2, 7, 8, 22, 43
    dance, dancing 109–11
    see also Carmen Olsson
periodic time 77, 83, 85, 148–9
periodicity 148
Perloff, Marjorie 8, 22
Petrarcha 117, 152
    Petrarchan sonnet 40–5, 117, 118
phenomenological process 39, 65
phonemes 44, 73
phrasal focus 58
phrase 47, 75–6, 81, 142–3, 151–2
    speech phrase 30–1
phrase rhythm 21, 23, 47, 58, 106, 126

Piaget, Jean 52, 63
pictorial poems 54–7
pitch 1–2, 95, 121, 127, 129, 134–6
Plath, Sylvia 22–5, 53, 56, 57–62
    see also Hughes
Plato 51, 109
*Playing by Ear and the Tip of the Tongue* (Tsur) 73
poem in the body 101–12
poetic gestalt 15–86
    cognitive versification theory 63–74
    levels and times 75–86
    rhythm and significance 39–49
    rhythmic gestalt 27–38
    temporal and spatial rhythms 51–62
    verse/versification systems 17–25
Pope, Alexander 97–8
Pöppel, Ernst 27, 30, 43, 46, 81, 90, 104
'Poppies in October' (Plath) 56, 57–62
*Prägnanz* 30
precategorical information, perception 72–4
preference rules 52
premodal patterning 72–3
premodality 52–4, 73–4
pressure *see* gestalt pressure
primary process 148
principle of equivalence 38
principle of rhythm
    dynamic rhythm 17, 18, 69, 103, 116
    sequential rhythm 17, 19, 21, 69, 103, 104, 116, 117
    serial rhythm 17, 18, 24, 25, 46, 68, 69, 76, 80, 103, 105, 116
print picture, printed picture 1, 51, 53, 59, 60, 62, 69, 72, 75, 118, 142, 143
    balance 142–3
    cognitive versification theory 69, 72
    levels and times 75
    *mousikē* 1
    patterns of culture 118
    temporal and spatial rhythms 51, 53, 59–60, 62
prolongation 6, 151
    anticipation 24, 107, 108, 128
    extension 24, 65, 71, 104, 107, 108, 128, 133
    goal 24, 64, 65, 69, 70, 71, 78, 84, 85, 107, 111, 126, 128, 140

promenade metaphors 125–6
proportion 9, 45, 139, 153
    see also temporality
proximity, law of 28–9
Psaltar rhythms 22, 136
psychological time 82–3, 84, 133
pulse/heart beats 46, 101–2, 103, 105, 110, 116

quantitative metre 19–20
quantitative verse system 6–7
Quintilianus 113

reading direction *see* direction
reduction process of cognitive economy 97–8
'Reflections on Vers Libre' (Eliot) 91, 92
Renaissance 6, 19, 20–1, 113–14, 122–3
repetition 2, 8, 11, 63–4, 154
    balance 143, 146, 147–50
    cognitive economy 91, 93, 94–5, 96, 99
    cognitive versification theory 63, 65, 71
    direction 128, 130–3, 136
    how to balance 143, 146
    levels and times 76, 79, 80–1, 83, 85–6
    patterns of culture 114, 121–2
    rhythm and significance 48–9
    rhythmic gestalt 29, 34–8
    rising/falling rhythm 132
    temporal and spatial rhythms 61
    verse systems/principles of rhythm 23–5
    see also rhyme
rhetoric 45, 113, 139
rhyme 7, 11, 20, 23–4
    end rhyme 79, 94, 146, 149
    levels and times 85
    patterns of culture 117, 118
        Paul Muldoon 117, 118–23
        rules and expressivity 123
    rhythmic gestalt 29, 38
rhythm schema 151
rhythm and significance 36–8, 39–49
rhythmic gestalt 27–38
    old and new phrases 30–1
    patterned line 27–30
    in versification 28–30
rhythmical principle, verse principle 17–19

*rhythmos* 9
Rimbaud, Arthur 69
rising rhythm 14, 49, 56, 128–33
Roman history 118–23
Romanticism 19, 20–1
rondeaux 113–14
rules and expressivity 123–4
*rune metre* 132
run-on lines 134

Sappho 7, 116, 152
Scandinavian poetry 22, 115
schema
    BALANCE schema 64–5, 67–70, 72, 111
    'Blockage' schema 70–1
    cognitive schema 54, 63, 64–7, 69
    'Compulsion' schema 71
    DIRECTION schema 64–5, 67–70
    FORCE schema 67–72, 125–8, 133, 135, 140, 151
    line schema 118, 122
    perceptual schema 63, 152
    rhythm schema 151
scientific time 56, 82–4, 131
secondary process 148
secondary stress 96, 98
segment, segmentation 11, 13, 18, 19, 54, 142
semantic direction 59
semantic field 152
semantic level 59
semantic rhythm 17, 69
semantic weight 140
semiotic text 39
semiotics 4, 39, 44, 53, 126, 131
sensorimotor
    cognitive schema 54, 63–7, 69
    experiences 46–7, 63–5, 103, 109, 152
    impulses 45
    sensorimotor-emotive process 52
sensory cortex 101
sequence 1, 4, 10, 17, 18, 19, 23, 24, 25, 27, 42, 45, 46, 54, 67, 89, 95, 97, 103, 111, 126, 129, 143
sequential rhythm 17, 19, 21, 69, 103, 104, 116, 117
serial rhythm 17, 18, 24, 25, 46, 68, 69, 76, 80, 103, 105, 116

seriality 18–19
*sestina* 117
sextets 117
Sexton, Anne 31–8, 126–35
Shakespeare, William 117
short syllables *see* weak syllables
short-term memory
    balance 146
    cognitive economy 90
    cognitive versification theory 73–4
    direction 133
    enjambment 133
    levels and times 75, 81
    poem in the body 103–4, 105
    rhythm and significance 46–7
    rhythmic gestalt 27, 30
    temporal and spatial rhythms 52
sign *see* semiotics
significance, signification 24–5, 39–49, 56, 97–9, 152
silent knowledge 74
similarity 85, 148
    law of 28–9
simplicity 90
'Sloe Gin' (Heaney) 104, 105–6
Snorri Sturluson 152
societal time 82
sonata 91
sonnet 113–14, 117–23
    Petrarchan 40–5, 117, 118
sound poems 8
sound repetition 85, 114
spatial art forms 3–4, 9, 139
spatial reading 11, 151
spatiality, spatial rhythm 11, 153
    *see also* temporality
speech phrase 30–1
speech rhythm 11, 13
    balance 141, 147, 151
    cognitive economy 91–2
    cognitive versification theory 67
    levels and times 76
    patterns of culture 117, 122–3
        rules and expressivity 123–4
    poem in the body 106, 108–9
    verse systems/principles of rhythm 22
spiral movement 132

spiral time *see* periodic time
Spitzer, Manfred
    cognitive versification theory 45–6, 63, 74
    levels and times 82
    poem in the body 104–5, 109
spondee 2, 7, 14
stability 3
    balance 3, 128
    direction 128, 138
stanza 47, 75–6, 81, 142–3, 151–2
    four-line stanza 42–3, 106
*strambotto* 117
stress *see* prominence
stress-timed metre 115
strong gestalts 99
subconscious 65, 102
subtext 34, 35, 80, 122
surrealism 136
syllabic verse system, syllabism 8
syllable stress ratios (SSR) 14
    balance in versification 144, 146–7
    patterns of culture 120–1
    rhythm and significance 47–8
    rhythmic gestalt 32–3, 36–7
    temporal and spatial rhythms 59
syllables 2, 5, 7, 8, 11–14
    balance 140–1, 144, 146
    cognitive economy 89, 90, 94, 96, 98, 99
    direction 128–31, 133, 134
    how to balance 146
    levels and times 79, 80
    long 31, 37, 113
    patterns of culture 113–17, 120–1
    poem in the body 104, 106, 109
    rhythm and significance 42–3, 46–9
    rhythmic gestalt 27–37
    short or weak 19, 30–1
    temporal and spatial rhythms 58, 59, 62
    verse systems/principles of rhythm 19–22
syllabomelodic verse 17
symmetric, asymmetric 10, 128, 143, 145
synaesthesia 45
synchrony 52

tactility, tactile 53
tactus 6, 9, 11, 13, 151
    cognitive economy 90, 94–8
    cognitive versification theory 63, 67–8
    direction 128–33
    domination of 116–17
    levels and times 76, 78, 79–80
    patterns of culture 114–17, 121–2, 123
    poem in the body 101, 103, 105
    rhythm and significance 40, 42, 46, 48, 49
    rhythmic gestalt 34
    verse systems/principles of rhythm 17–21, 23, 24
tempo 12, 80, 84
    balance in versification 147, 149
    cognitive economy 94
    cognitive versification theory 69
    direction 129–32, 136
    poem in the body 105
    rhythmic gestalt 34–9
    *see also* time
temporal art forms 3–4, 9, 17–18, 52–3, 111
temporal and spatial rhythms 56, 58–9, 61–2
temporal lobe 46
temporal rhythm 1, 53
temporality 51–62
    *see also* spatiality
tension 72
tensions, dynamic 54
terza rima 33, 35
terzet 117
three-beat line 20
three-second intervals 46, 81, 103, 109
tightrope walking 10, 71, 110, 139
timbre 39
time arrow 128–9, 133, 153
time 75, 81–6, 133, 143, 153
    *see also* repetitions
timescape 82–3
tirade 43
Tranströmer, Tomas 45
tribrach 121, 146
trochee 130–1
    direction 129, 131–3
    rhythmic gestalt 34
    temporal and spatial rhythms 56

Tsur, Reuven 4–6, 9–11, 13, 21
    balance in versification 139, 147–8, 150
    cognitive economy 89–99
    cognitive versification theory 63, 64, 71–4
    direction 128, 129, 131, 133, 134
    patterns of culture 117, 123
    poem in the body 104, 105, 107–8
    rhythm and significance 39, 40, 43–8
    rhythmic gestalt 28–30, 32, 34, 35, 36, 38
    rising/falling rhythm 129, 131
    temporal and spatial rhythms 52–4
twin pan balance 141–3
typography 24, 54–6

'Unique Forms of Continuity' (Boccioni) 136, 137
unity 28
universal interval 104
unmarked *see* marked

verse history 6, 19
verse systems 6–7, 8, 13
    accentual verse 5, 6, 20, 21
    four-beat line xiv, 5, 7, 20, 21, 22, 29, 30, 42, 66, 90–96, 103, 104, 106, 115, 116, 118, 123
    quantitative metre 19
    syllabism 8, 21, 115
    syllabomelodic verse 17
versification systems 2, 4–5, 6–10, 13
    avant-garde 7, 8, 22
    balance 139–50
    cognitive economy 90–2
    direction 127, 128–9, 133, 136
    levels and times 84
    patterns of culture 114, 116, 118, 123–4
    poem in the body 101, 103, 105–6
    rhythm and significance 42, 44–6
    rhythmic gestalt 27, 28–30, 31
    temporal and spatial rhythms 51, 56, 60–1
    *see also* verse systems
villanelles 113–14
visuality, visual rhythm 51, 52, 69–72, 143
*volta* (turn) 117, 118, 121
    Muldoon's sonnet 118–19

walking 102, 105–11, 125
    tightrope walking 10, 71, 110, 139
    *see also* biorhythms
'The Waste Land' (Eliot) 92
weak gestalts 99
weak syllables 2, 5, 8–9, 12–14
    balance 140
    cognitive economy 96, 98
    direction 128, 129
    patterns of culture 115–16
    poem in the body 104
    rhythmic gestalt 30
    temporal and spatial rhythms 58
    verse systems/principles of rhythm 20
weight 59, 130–1, 140
Wertheimer, Max 28–9
Whitman, Walt 8, 138
whole poem 47, 75–6, 81, 142–3, 151–2
'Winter Trees' (Plath) 22–5
Wittgenstein, Ludwig 64
working songs 20

www.ingramcontent.com/pod-product-compliance
Lightning Source LLC
Chambersburg PA
CBHW052046300426
44117CB00012B/1992